Willy Ley, who was born in Berlin, Germany, in 1906, studied at the Universities of Berlin and Königsberg in East Prussia, concentrating on paleontology, astronomy, and physics. He was, from his early high school days, fascinated not only by all aspects of scientific fact, but by the history behind scientific discoveries. This interest in scientific history, as Ley readers can attest, is one of the unique features of his books. Willy Ley had planned to be a geologist until he read the fundamental book on rocket theory by Professor Hermann Oberth in 1925 and became interested in the theoretical work being done on rockets and space travel. In 1927 he became one of the founders (and later was vice-president) of the German Rocket Society, which pioneered in rocket research. From that time on his interest in rockets has been alternately his profession or his hobby, depending on circumstances.

In 1935, after the advent of Hitler, Willy Ley left Germany for an "extended vacation" in England. He arrived in the United States later that year, and is now an American citizen, living in New York City with his wife and two daughters. He served as science editor for the New York newspaper *PM,* a research engineer for the Washington (D.C.) Institute of Technology, and consultant to the Office of Technical Services of the Department of Commerce. He is now professor of science at Fairleigh Dickinson University in New Jersey and lectures widely on current projects of the space program.

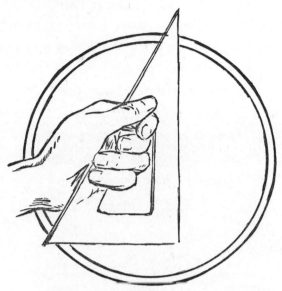

Engineers' Dreams

BY WILLY LEY

Diagrams and maps by Willy Ley

Illustrations by Isami Kashiwagi

REVISED EDITION

THE VIKING PRESS

New York

LIBRARY OF CONGRESS CATALOG CARD NUMBER: 54-5683

PRINTED IN THE U.S.A. BY THE VAIL-BALLOU PRESS, INC.

Contents

Illustrations

*(Maps and diagrams by Willy Ley; all other illustrations
by Isami Kashiwagi)*

7

Foreword to the First Edition

Engineers' dreams are things that can be done—as far as the engineer is concerned. They are also things that cannot be done —for reasons that have nothing to do with engineering. Sometimes it is a question of money: the sums involved may be so huge that only government could pay them; or commercial interests may not be convinced that the project is worth the expenditure. In some cases there may be a clash of interests.

But many—in fact the majority—of engineers' dreams are still dreams, and may stay in that stage, because of political difficulties. Engineering projects are based on natural facts—say, the outline of a bay or a valley or the course of a river. Political boundaries are sometimes based on similar facts but as a rule they are the result of historical developments, with a good deal of chance thrown in, and the political boundary may cut across the project area. If this does not kill the project outright it results in a mountain of paperwork that is far harder to get out of the way than a real mountain of mere rock would be.

A few cases are what might be called incompleted dreams, ideas that are clear enough in outline but with something still lacking, a survey to be completed, a development still to be made, or a thought to be finished.

The accounts in this book do not by any means exhaust the subject. There are scores and scores, or, more likely, hundreds and hundreds, of such unfinished projects in existence. Nor should any of these accounts be taken as a "prediction." No prediction that this or that will be done is possible; there are too many highly uncertain factors involved. But just because these factors are so uncertain they may shift around and all of a sudden favor something which was formerly politically impossible, or economically impracticable, or even thought to be obsolete. In short, the following chapters do not tell what will be done, nor even what should be done, but merely what could be done.

What *will* happen must be left to the future.

WILLY LEY

New York City, October 1953

Foreword to the Revised Edition

Since the end of 1953 when this book was first published—in the meantime it has been translated into quite a number of foreign languages, including Arabic, Dutch, French, and Polish—none of the projects described here has actually been realized, but some of them have progressed somewhat closer toward realization.

Two new chapters have been added, both dealing with projects underway: one about the successful struggle of the Dutch to increase their land area, and the other about the Greater Volga Plan of the Russians.

The next decade is likely to bring the realization of a few of these projects, and probably a dozen new dreams.

WILLY LEY

New York City, January 1964

1. FORBIDDEN TUNNEL

1. How the mouth of the Channel Tunnel would look.

Forbidden Tunnel

As the nineteenth century drew to its close and people began to take stock of what had happened, they realized that they could look back proudly at a whole century of startling progress, characterized by a large number of fundamental and to them almost unbelievable inventions.

The development had begun with the steam engine, which at first was a clumsy and ponderous beast, used mostly to pump water from mines and not much good for anything else. In the course of the century it had become less clumsy and was no longer excessively ponderous; in fact, it could almost be called agile. The locomotive had moved in where the horse had formerly dragged flimsy cars along wooden rails, and the travel time between any two cities had been halved and then halved again. On the seas, sails had given way to smokestacks; steam had conquered first the Atlantic and then the other oceans, likewise halving and again halving travel times.

At the beginning of the century messages had to go by dispatch rider (and in exceptional cases by carrier pigeon), but only a few decades later the electric telegraph ruled communications, even across the ocean. And during the last years of the century there were discussions on whether the newly developed telephone might, in time, infringe upon the telegraph's monopoly. A few people, pointing to the experiments performed by one Heinrich Hertz involving "electromagnetic waves" (whatever they might be), even predicted that there might some day be a telegraph that did not require wires to connect the cities. Such speculations were of course called "fantastic"—people at the end of the nineteenth century had not yet learned that the word fantastic, when applied to engineering, merely means "it has not yet been done."

In the course of the century photography had been invented, the candle had been replaced by gaslight, and gaslight itself had engaged in a losing battle with electric illumination. Aluminum moved in where tin, copper, and brass had been the only alternatives to iron. Dynamite and other high explosives took over where blackpowder would not do. Synthetic dyes began to be successful. But the people of, say, 1898 did not feel much pride about that development. Nor were they very proud of a few other promising beginnings. Some submarines had been built, yes, but they usually drowned their crews. One Dr. Rudolf Diesel had invented an interesting new engine, but they had the steam engine and electric motors, so why complicate matters? "Horseless carriages" of several kinds were being tried, but still were not taken seriously. A few "dirigible balloons" had taken to the air, but strictly in good weather. Otto Lilienthal of Germany had shown that one could fly in an unpowered airplane, but in the end he had been killed in a crash.

What people *were* proud of, in addition to trains and long telegraph lines, were the big construction projects. In 1862 a bridge more than 1000 feet long had been built near Wheeling, West Virginia. Only one year later the Ohio River was spanned at Cincinnati by a bridge 40 feet longer than the Wheeling bridge—1050 feet long. In 1883 the "East River Bridge" (now known as the Brooklyn Bridge) was completed, spanning just under 1600 feet. Seven years later the British completed an even longer bridge, the one across the Firth of Forth in Scotland, which is 1710 feet long.

During the same years in which this tall bridge rose, an even taller structure began to sprout from the Champs de Mars in Paris—the 984-foot tower of Monsieur Alexandre Gustave Eiffel. At first many Parisians were not in the least proud of this structure; it was publicly denounced as an eyesore and a useless one to boot.

But there was unanimous pride in the long canals. The Greeks had their Corinth Canal, only 4 miles long but very useful. The Dutch had their 15½-mile Amsterdam Canal and the English their 35-mile Manchester Canal. Of course all these were overshadowed in fame, size, and usefulness by the somewhat older Suez Canal, more than 100 miles long, which saved a 15,000-mile voyage around Africa.

If people, in thinking back about their accomplishments during the nineteenth century, had any regrets, these were for two projects dear to their hearts which had not yet come to pass. One was the canal across the isthmus of Central America, which had had to be abandoned for financial reasons; however, nobody doubted that it would be built in the near future. The other project, the one most Europeans considered would be the crowning achievement of many decades of progress, was the dry-land link between England and continental Europe: the railroad tunnel from Calais to Dover. The public in England referred to it as the Channel Tunnel, the public in France called it *tunnel sous la Manche,* and both wanted it. The engineers had drawn their plans with great enthusiasm, and the public had invested its pounds and francs with even greater enthusiasm. But the project had run into political difficulties. These, though not completely unforeseen, had not been considered very serious, and still seemed merely a postponement. Countless newspaper editors, writing century-end round-up articles, expressed confidence that the political difficulties opposing the Channel Tunnel would be overcome, just as the financial difficulties of the Panama Canal project could be solved somehow.

The Panama Canal was finished a decade and a half later, but the Channel Tunnel is still only a project.

The geographical situation is simplicity itself. Even the most casual glance at a map shows that the large island of Great Britain almost touches the European mainland at one point. They come together most closely in the areas between Dover and Folkestone on the English side, and between Calais and Cape Gris Nez on the French side. The English Channel is called the Strait of Dover at that point and is about 21 miles wide from land to land. On a clear day you can see across it; the famed white cliffs of Dover are matched by similar chalk cliffs on the French side.

As recently as 15,000 years ago the Strait of Dover did not exist. Great Britain was a 90,000-square-mile promontory of western Europe. The western portion of the Channel was a bay; so was the whole North Sea. The sea broke through and made Great Britain into an island only a few thousand years before civilization's history began at the eastern end of the Mediterranean. The Strait of Dover is not only narrow, it is also not very deep; at low tide the bottom of the strait is only 165 feet below the surface.

The thought of connecting the two headlands by a tunnel cropped up a good many years before it was possible to do the job. The original father of the idea was a French engineer named Mathieu-Favier. He wrote a report about his plan, which involved the creation of a small island near the center of the strait, where a shoal rises to within 100 feet of the surface. Tunnels were to go to this island from either side, each tunnel about a dozen miles long. With horse-drawn cars running on rails each tunnel trip would require about an hour—or a little more than 2 hours would be required for the whole trip from France to England.

Engineer Mathieu-Favier submitted his report to the First Consul of the French Republic, a gentleman by the name of Napoleon Bonaparte. The year was 1802.

Napoleon was impressed. At the earliest opportunity he discussed the plan with the English statesman Charles James Fox. "Think," he said, "what great things we could do together." Fox replied politely and diplomatically that "a Franco-British union could rule the world." Whether Fox actually liked the plan is not certain, but even if he had there was little he could have done. To say that his relations with the king of England were strained is putting things politely. Moreover, the peace between England and France was in itself precarious. Only a few years after that conversation, Napoleon looked across the Channel at "the enemy" and held discussions with his generals on how to get an army across the water and onto English soil.

We now know—which Mathieu-Favier did not—that the conditions for a tunnel from Cape Gris Nez to Folkestone are about as favorable as possible. The headlands on both sides rest on a solid layer of grayish chalk several hundred feet thick. It has been named the Lower Gray Chalk, because there are two other layers of chalk above it which are known as the Upper Chalk and the Middle Chalk. The Lower Gray Chalk is soft enough to be worked without blasting. More important, it is impermeable to water: a hole drilled through it will stay dry, except for moisture that may be carried in by air. Most important, it stretches all the way across and there is no reason to suppose that it is broken or discontinued anywhere within that 21-mile stretch.

Still, if Napoleon's war engineers had actually gone to work on Mathieu-Favier's plan, probably it would have had to be abandoned. It is highly doubtful that the French could have built an artificial island, 130 feet deep and some 800 feet in circumference, without power machinery, or that the two 12-mile tunnels could have been dug with pickaxes and hand drills. Finally, even if everything had somehow worked out, there would have been the problem of ventilation, which needs plenty of power, especially if illumination is furnished by oil-burning wicks. Mathieu-Favier's plan was unworkable as it stood, but the idea took hold immediately and has never been given up since.

During the decades immediately following the first proposal a number of engineers, both French and English, toyed with the idea of a tunnel that could be manufactured and would not have to be dug. You can lay an iron pipe across a river, resting it on the bottom. Why not a pipe large enough to drive through, across the bottom of the Strait of Dover? The first to propose this idea seems to have been a Frenchman named Tessier de

Mottray. An English engineer named Dunn—who may or may not have known of the Frenchman's suggestion—advocated the same plan, complete with calculations on how strong the tube would have to be to stand the water pressure at a depth of 160 feet. When critics pointed out that the bottom of the Channel is not, after all, as smooth as a roadbed, the English engineer James Wylson introduced a variation. He did not want his pipe to rest on the bottom directly but on supports of varying lengths so that the "tunnel" would run in a straight line at a uniform depth of, say, 80 feet all the way. This involved the extra expense of building supports, but would avoid ups and downs in the tube. Besides, the tube would not have to be quite so strong since it would have to stand far less water pressure.

As a matter of fact, such a tube would not need "supporting" as much as "tying down," for an air-filled pipe 10 or 12 feet in diameter would be quite buoyant. If it were assembled by men in diving suits and were full of water while under construction it would exhibit a strong tendency to break away from its moorings when pumped dry.

Between these proposals came one from two Frenchmen, Ransonnet and Polonçeau, to dispense with a tunnel, whether dug or manufactured, and to span the Channel with a bridge. The reasoning seems to have been that, while building a bridge, one is at least out in the open air and can see what is going on. And engineers certainly had more experience with bridges than with tunnels—remember that diving suits as we know them did not exist a century ago. Ransonnet and Polonçeau even estimated the cost: the 24-mile-long bridge would have cost about 4000 million gold francs. When everybody shook his head upon hearing this sum, they revised their plans. Instead of a bridge they advocated a dam which was to have three wide gaps for ships to pass through. These gaps were to be spanned by high bridges. Estimated cost: 840 million gold francs.

Even now it may seem at first glance that either a tunnel assembled of lengths of pipe of the proper size and tied to supports which smooth out the irregularities of the bottom, or a dam with bridged gaps, would be a less difficult job than a continuous tunnel with a total length of 30 miles, counting the approaches on both sides. Actually the true tunnel, if you have the mechanical means for digging it, is the simplest and consequently the least expensive solution. The tubular tunnel and also the interrupted dam present considerable difficulties while under construction. The problem is that for either you have to work half in and half out of the water, hampered by winds, waves, and currents. And the weather over the English Channel is changeable, to say the least; strong winds occur frequently, and at some times of the year fog is virtually constant. If you dig a true tunnel, no kind of weather can interfere; the problems are merely ventilation and removal of the debris.

The first man to realize this clearly and to say so was a Frenchman, Thomé de Gamond, who for the whole second half of the nineteenth century was the chief advocate of the Channel Tunnel idea. Born in 1807, Thomé de Gamond received an exceptional education; he was a doctor, a lawyer, and an engineer, but mostly an engineer. As a student he met and made friends with Prince Louis Napoleon; at a later date he formed a friendship with Ferdinand de Lesseps, who was just two years his senior, and in 1831–32 accompanied him to Egypt. There de Lesseps conceived the idea of connecting the Mediterranean and the Red Sea with a canal—the Suez Canal, which he later built.

While building the Suez Canal he looked at maps of Central America and dreamed of still another great canal, which he actually started at a later date, but did not finish.

While his friend de Lesseps dreamed of watery connections between bodies of water, Thomé de Gamond thought about the land connection between France and England, the tunnel which his compatriot Mathieu-Favier had first conceived half a century earlier. In 1856, when his old friend Louis Napoleon sat on the restored throne of France as Emperor Napoleon III, de Gamond presented him with a plan for a Channel Tunnel. The political atmosphere was good, and not only because the emperor and the engineer had known each other for a long time. Napoleon III was in the habit of doing everything that he thought his uncle Napoleon I would have done. In regard to the Channel Tunnel he did not even have to figure out what Napoleon I *would* have done. The first Napoleon's elation with the idea was a matter of historical record, so Napoleon III unhesitatingly supported de Gamond's plan. To smooth the way even further, Napoleon III happened to be on better terms with England than any other French ruler for many centuries had been. He had lived in exile in England for years; he had made France join England in the Crimean War against Russia. The English considered him very much a "neighbor and ally."

But the first proposal made by de Gamond did not find many friends, most of the resistance coming from seafaring people. The plan called not just for one but for thirteen artificial islands in the Channel. They were supposed to serve a double purpose. Essentially they were to be dumping places for the material excavated under the bottom. But each artificial island was to contain a "chimney," a connection between the tunnel and the fresh air above, in order to facilitate ventilation. Maritime circles told de Gamond, and anybody else who would listen, that navigation across and through the Channel was difficult enough, what with frequent storms and fog and rain, and that thirteen artificial islands would add thirteen obstacles to make the sailor's life even more difficult. Islands, natural or otherwise, might be acceptable elsewhere but not between England and France. "The English Channel," one sea captain is said to have exclaimed, "is not the Gulf of Mexico!" There was even some political opposition. Lord Palmerston, the British Prime Minister, said bluntly to de Gamond, "How can you expect us to further reduce a distance which is too short as it is?"

Thomé de Gamond paid little attention to this attitude, but he heeded the nautical objections and set about revising his plans. It was obviously necessary to dig the tunnel from both ends without the aid of intermediate stations. The difficulty was, over long distances, to get fresh air in and debris out, all through the same hole. But here experience gathered by English mining engineers proved to be helpful. They had had a similar problem in coal mining (where thorough ventilation is even more important to avoid coal-gas explosions) and had solved it by digging their tunnels in pairs, with frequent cross connections. After 10 years of work, which also involved testing the bottom of the Channel for continuity of the chalk strata, Thomé de Gamond finished an improved version of his original scheme.

In 1868 the Anglo-French Tunnel Committee was formed. It included Thomé de Gamond, the Scottish engineer William Lowe, the English engineers Joseph Lock and Robert Stephenson, and Isambard Brunel, who was something of a connecting link, being an English engineer of French ancestry. (His father, also an engineer, had fled the French Revolution as a young man.) Somewhat later Sir John Hawkshaw became a member. By that time the political situation was even better; the Anglo-French treaty from Crimean War times still held, and the skeptical Lord Palmerston had died. William E. Gladstone was Prime Minister, and he favored the tunnel. So did Lord Lansdowne and Lord Salisbury. So did Queen Victoria, who received de Gamond at Buckingham Palace. Emperor Napoleon III also gave a large reception for the Tunnel Committee.

Any project of such a size requires a long organizational period. A complete set of engineering plans is only the veriest beginning. Before much could be done in addition to statements of good will and official favor, the Franco-Prussian War of 1870–71 began. The war did not last long, but it cost Napoleon III his throne, and France became a republic once more. But even though an imperial protector was now lacking, the war did not constitute a setback for the Channel Tunnel. The official creation of the German Reich at the end of that war caused France and England to look toward each other for mutual assistance against Germany. A convention between Queen Victoria's government and the French Republic, to regulate Channel Tunnel problems which would arise, was signed in 1875. In both countries companies for financing the work were formed.

The French had always felt that the Channel Tunnel was really theirs, most of the plans having originated in France. They were perfectly willing to finance the tunnel themselves and they had the necessary capital. The French company (called Comité Français du Tunnel) was backed by the House of Rothschild and by a railroad company, the Chemins de Fer du Nord, aided and abetted by the Suez Canal Company which had found out at

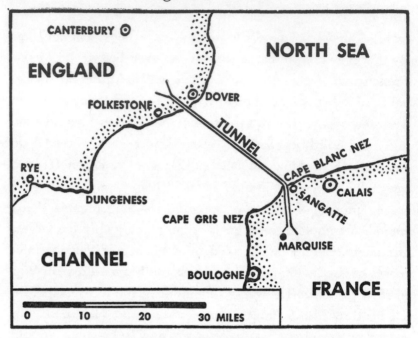

2. The projected path of the Channel Tunnel

first hand how profitable it can be to back a large and novel engineering project. But the English did not wish to be left out of the financial end either; what complicated the picture on the English side was that two railroad companies which were competing with each other anyway also competed for the financing of the tunnel. Three different companies were formed in England, but they merged after some time. The result was the Channel Tunnel Company, headed by Sir David Watkins, Lord Richard Grosvenor, and William Lowe. Its money—a quarter-million pounds—had come from London financiers and from the South Eastern Railway Company.

In 1877 the companies submitted to their respective governments the final plan as drawn up by the three chief engineers,

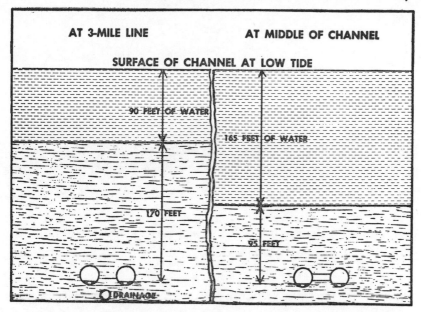

AT 3-MILE LINE   AT MIDDLE OF CHANNEL

SURFACE OF CHANNEL AT LOW TIDE

90 FEET OF WATER

165 FEET OF WATER

170 FEET

95 FEET

DRAINAGE

3. Thomé de Gamond's twin tunnels, near the shore and in the middle of the English Channel—latest revised version

Sir John Hawkshaw, Sir James Brunlees, and Thomé de Gamond. De Gamond had died the year before, but his death, though mourned, had not appreciably delayed the work.

The tunnel, when completed, was to be a twin tunnel with circular cross sections, each 20 feet in diameter. The two tunnels were to have cross connections every 350 feet; their length under the bottom of the Channel was to be a fraction over 20 miles, with a 4-mile approach at each end. The British approach was to begin behind the Dover cliffs and descend sharply to a depth of 250 feet below sea level. From then on the descent was to be more gradual, reaching its greatest depth of about 300 feet below sea level not quite 5 miles from the shore. From there the tunnel was to rise very gently so that it would be some 200

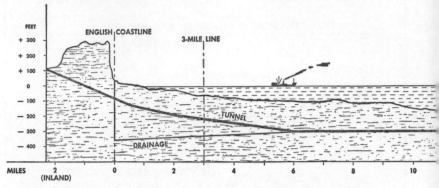

4. The bed of the English Channel, showing the proposed tunnel of the Channel Tunnel Railroad, Ltd.

feet below sea level 2½ miles from the French shore. It was to emerge at the French end behind Cape Blanc Nez and terminate at Marquise, a small town halfway between Calais and Boulogne. The reason the tunnel was not planned to be quite horizontal is simple: a perfectly horizontal tunnel would be hard to keep dry, since moisture would have a tendency to accumulate in the center. If the tunnel slanted just a bit one way or another, the moisture would run to the deepest point and drain into a third tube, smaller than the other two, with a diameter of 5 or 6 feet, which was called the "drainage heading." Near the shores this drainage heading would run far below the tunnel proper, being 400 feet below sea level at the French shore line and almost that deep below the English shore line. At these two points, Sangatte in France and Shakespeare Cliff in England, the drainage heading was to be tapped by vertical shafts through which the water could be pumped out and discharged into the Channel.

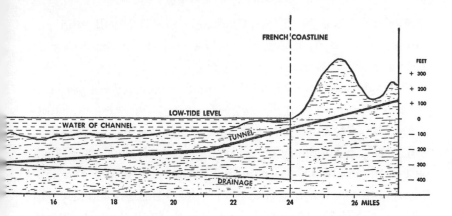

The water which was to be taken care of by the drainage heading and ultimately by the pumps at Sangatte and Shakespeare Cliff would not be seepage from the Channel but merely moisture which would enter the tunnel with the air and condense inside. None of the engineers expected any seepage, for even in the middle of the Channel there would be some 90 feet of waterproof gray chalk between the tunnel and the bottom of the Channel, and at other points there would be even twice as much.

Actual work began around 1880 with the sinking of two vertical shafts at the foot of Shakespeare Cliff and at Sangatte. These shafts were to house the pumping ducts later; at first they were to serve as bases for drilling test tunnels under the Channel bed. The French test tunnel was 4800 feet long; the English test tunnel, built under the supervision of William Lowe, had a length of 6500 feet. Visitors to these test tunnels were greatly impressed by the electric illumination, and by the hand-drawn trolley cars in which they could ride. Most of the visitors were certainly important personages: Queen Victoria and the Prince of Wales, Prime Ministers Gladstone and Disraeli, and apparently everybody else with enough position or reputation to wangle an invitation.

The main work of digging the tunnel proper had not yet been started. Engineers and geologists were still checking and testing as the pilot tunnels lengthened. What was being done was still largely preliminary work, even though all of it would be a part of the final tunnel system. But preliminary or not, the public on both sides of the Channel followed the news avidly and with expectations. The whole project would take between 6 and 8 years, the engineers had said. Therefore in 1888, or at the latest in 1890, French businessmen and English tourists reasoned, one would be able to make the trip to London—or to Paris—comfortably in a train, possibly asleep. No need then for getting up in the middle of the night to climb the gangplank of a Channel steamer in pouring rain—ending up seasick, more likely than not!

Those who were well informed had known all along that the entire English nation was not as unanimously in favor of the tunnel as the French were. The Queen favored it, yes; her Prime Minister, yes. Large sections of the House of Commons, of course. And many members of the House of Lords as well. Here and there, of course, were individuals who disapproved of the scheme, but about the only group that was definitely opposed as a group was the British War Office. In 1882 the War Office struck. The *Times* of London all of a sudden published a strongly worded editorial opposing the completion of the tunnel. Not on grounds of unexpected technical or financial difficulties— the *Times* attacked the idea itself. England would no longer be an island if the tunnel were completed.

During the same year Lord Wolseley, British Chief of Staff, issued a blue book denouncing the tunnel as a military liability. If allowed to exist it would "constitute a permanent menace to England's security." He listed four possibilities. First, by means of the tunnel England could be invaded without declaration of war by a surprise action, probably by troops disguised as tourists using the tunnel trains. Second, the British end of the tunnel might be captured by a surprise attack with troops which had been landed by sea near Folkestone, and after the British end was in the enemy's hands the tunnel trains could bring in the invading army. Third, traitors might do the job for the enemy and turn the tunnel over to him at a prearranged time. Fourth, and finally, an enemy might win a war against England without recourse to the tunnel but ask for the tunnel as part of the peace terms afterward, thus rendering England permanently helpless.

Popular sentiment in England remained in favor of the tunnel, possibly because the average Englishman could deduce from Lord Wolseley's four points that the "enemy" could only be France, and to the average man the French did not really look like enemies. Nor did the French behave like enemies; Lord Wolseley's points could very easily have insulted them, but if they felt insulted they concealed it. However, an influential and popular magazine called *The Nineteenth Century* sided with the *Times* and collected a number of famous men who were willing to speak out against the tunnel. The Duke of Wellington joined hands with the philosopher Herbert Spencer, the poet Robert Browning, and the scientist Thomas Huxley, with the Duke of Marlborough at the other end of the anti-tunnel chain. From the point of view of the reader of seventy years later they all talked hopeless nonsense, but it probably sounded like profound reasoning then.

After a speech by Lord Wolseley to the House of Lords the matter was referred to a mixed commission of ten members of both houses of Parliament, with Lord Lansdowne as chairman. Lord Lansdowne was still in favor of the tunnel, and there were lengthy debates. Finally the matter came to a vote (July 10, 1883), and six members of the commission voted against the tunnel, only three siding with Lord Lansdowne. The French pointed out with much glee that the vote showed a most interesting weakness: the six members who had been against the tunnel could not agree on the reason for opposing it. The next step was that the Channel Tunnel Company, Ltd., was called upon to prove that an invasion of England could be prevented with absolute certainty even if the tunnel existed.

The suggestions made were the obvious ones: a special citadel at the British end with artillery commanding the tunnel entrance; massive steel gates that could be dropped at various places along the sloping section of the tunnel and would at least delay an enemy; explosives planted in such a manner that a section of the tunnel (one which was already above sea level to facilitate later repairs) could be made to cave in. Lord Wolseley rejected each suggestion as "not foolproof," and unfortunately he could cite an example which was not too pleasing to the French. There existed several railroad tunnels through the Vosges mountains in the eastern part of France, and the French had mined these tunnels very carefully so that they could be collapsed in case of a war with the Germans. But when the war of 1870–71 began, the Frenchmen in charge of the mined tunnels could not decide whether or not the explosive charges should be ignited. The result of their hesitation was that the Germans captured the tunnels before the French made up their minds, and used them all through the war for their own supplies and replacements. This, Lord Wolseley insisted, could happen to the Channel Tunnel too.

In 1884 work at the British end was discontinued. The French, possibly in order to set an example, possibly out of sheer inertia, kept on for a while longer and then they too stopped the work. The Channel Tunnel project had been knocked out by Lord Wolseley.

Two decades later tunnel enthusiasts in both countries tried to revive the project, and the British statesman Lord Asquith admitted in 1904 that his personal opinion was "not unfriendly." But in 1906, when actual discussions began, the Prime Minister, Sir Henry Campbell-Bannermann, rejected the project, repeating everything Lord Wolseley had said and adding some dire predictions of his own. Lord Asquith, then Chancellor of the Exchequer, kept quiet or at least did not raise an issue, though he had said on an earlier occasion that a tunnel would be a nice thing to have in case of a sea blockade.

The next important date in the history of the Channel Tunnel is one which, at first glance, seems to be entirely unconnected. On July 25, 1909, the French aviator Louis Blériot took off from France, flew across the Channel, and landed in England. One year later, in 1910, the British government purchased the first British military airship from the brothers Paul and Pierre Lebaudy, who flew the ship across the Channel to England. Since the main argument all along had been that a tunnel would destroy England's insularity, the proponents of the tunnel had much reason to be happy. People had come to England in a

manner which the Royal Navy could not have stopped. With airplanes and airships insularity was a thing of the past. Maybe the
government would now permit the tunnel to be built for two
peacetime reasons: convenience and profits.

In 1913 Sir Francis Fox, a civil engineer who had built the
bridge across the Zambezi River at Victoria Falls and had tunnel
experience both in the London subway system and as consultant
for the Simplon Tunnel through the Alps, produced a revised
plan for the Channel Tunnel, worked out with Albert Sartinaux
of the French company. This plan had some variations from the
original. The tunnel followed a slightly different path which
was a few miles longer. The portion under the Channel bottom
was to be somewhat deeper down. The most important innova-
tion was that electricity was used not only for illumination but
to run the trains. The proposal almost received a majority in the
House of Commons—as the 1906 proposal had—but again it
was only almost a majority. Lord Asquith, then Prime Minister,
rejected it, and the London *Times* repeated the old argument
once more with the statement: "If we get a tunnel we also get
a dry border and our isolation is ended. . . . Such a project can
only be harmful."

Then came the First World War. Lord Wolseley had died in
1913 and did not see to what an incredible extent he had been
wrong. The "enemy" he had constantly invoked turned out to
be England's most reliable ally. London was bombed from the
air by German Zeppelin airships. German naval mines and German submarines did not "conquer" the seas around England but
they made them decidedly unsafe. How nice it would have been
to have had a continuous stream of trains going both ways along
a route which neither Zeppelins nor submarines could possibly

disturb. In 1916 a Member of Parliament, Sir Arthur Fell, said what many Englishmen felt: "The conduct of the war has shown the great advantages England and her allies would have drawn from the existence of a railroad under the Channel, and the time has come for the government to approve the project so that the work may be put in hand, after the war, as soon as the necessary workmen can be found."

Engineers made additional safety suggestions to quiet any fears that might be left. The tunnel trains and all the tunnel mechanisms could be operated on an unusual voltage which ordinary power plants do not deliver, and the special power plant for the whole would be in England. The British tunnel entrance could be a few miles farther inland than originally planned and could be ringed by special fortifications. The tunnel could have a "dip" over a mile long which could be flooded so that the tunnel could be made impassable without being destroyed. The whole tunnel could be filled with poison gas. The French stated that they would agree to all this if the English deemed it necessary. One French spokesman asked with a great show of innocence whether the British were sure that such precautions could really defend a mousehole and promised that the French, at their end, would be satisfied with a massive steel door of the type used for bank vaults, half a dozen field guns, and a few machine-gun emplacements.

It seemed certain then that the tunnel would be built after the war.

In 1920 the British government rejected the plan.

In 1924 the British government rejected the plan.

Ramsay MacDonald, then Prime Minister, called a conference of all former prime ministers still living. Lord Wolseley's ghost indubitably attended too. They met for 40 minutes and decided on rejection, even though the Members of Parliament supported the tunnel with a majority of two to one. Winston Churchill—not then in office—raised his voice. "There is no doubt about their promptitude. The question is: was their decision right or wrong? I do not hesitate to say that it was wrong."

It has never been disclosed just what the assembled former prime ministers discussed; most likely much of the debate hinged on how the outcome of the First World War would have been affected by the existence of the tunnel. Ferdinand Foch, marshal of France, and supreme commander of all the Allied Armies in World War I, had gone on record on that question in 1922: "If the Channel Tunnel had been built it might have prevented the war, and in any event it would have shortened its duration by one-half!" (The French tunnel company promptly elected him Honorary President after that speech.) But the prime ministers did not believe Foch.

In 1928 and 1929 debate flared up again—always in England, of course, for the French tunnel company has the approval of its government and can go ahead any time it wants to, but the English company cannot proceed without an Act of Parliament. The government of Stanley Baldwin, then England's Prime Minister, issued a blue book endorsing the tunnel but the War Office massed its literary guns, namely the *Army Quarterly* and the *Royal United Service Institutions Journal*. The *Army Quarterly* said little about the military aspects; there was no use denying the existence of airplanes and the fact that any big gun even then could easily shoot across the Channel. The *Army Quarterly* suddenly talked about money. People expected, it said, that the building of the tunnel would provide employment, either directly or through the purchase of materials, cement, steel, rails, electrical equipment. But the contracts would all go to the lowest bidders and, the *Army Quarterly* asserted, the low bids would come from any country except England. No doubt the tunnel companies would make money, but would England as a whole? Of course not. The tourists would all go one way, namely to France, since the French do not travel much, and the freight would all go the other way, since the English prefer French merchandise. In short, France would win and England would lose.

The *Royal United Service Institutions Journal* did present military arguments, or at least some double talk that sounded like arguments. Both Sir Archibald Hurd and Sir W. D. Bird declared that they did not like the tunnel, that its existence would diminish the pride of the British in being islanders. Sir Reginald H. S. Bacon declared that Marshal Foch had been wrong—if there had been a tunnel the German armies would have rushed for the tunnel instead of for Paris. He failed to mention that the German armies in the First World War did not capture Paris, and he concluded that in another war the Germans would "not repeat their old mistakes." This of course could only mean that it was a mistake of the German High Command that there was no tunnel for them to attack.

The article by Air Commodore J. A. Chamier indulged in a kind of "reasoning" which requires unusual powers of concentration to follow. The train-and-boat trip from London to Paris, he stated, normally takes about 7½ hours, counting 1½ hours for the actual Channel crossing and 1 hour for delays on both sides. With the tunnel the travel time would be reduced to "say 5½ hours" but this unimportant saving would have disastrous consequences. As things stand most people travel in daytime because of the interruption of their trip at the water's edge. With tunnel trains they would travel at night, in sleeping cars, preferring tunnel trains to airliners. But without extensive air travel you can't have an air-minded population; "therefore the tunnel constitutes a very serious menace to the growth of civil aviation." And with less civilian interest in flying fewer young men would feel inclined to join the Royal Air Force, and as a result England's military air strength would diminish to the point of helplessness.

After your breathing has returned to normal you may consider one more argument, this one a little more sound. Channel boats of assorted sizes carry the supplies on which England depends. If the freight were handled by tunnel trains the number of these boats would decrease, and in time of war, with the tunnel inoperative, it would be hard to get the necessary number of boats back into service quickly enough.

At that point a Swiss engineer named Julius Jaeger stepped in with a proposal which would provide train travel across the Channel, plus freight boat service, plus perfect military control of the whole installation at any moment. Jaeger actually revived the old French suggestion of a Channel dam, but with a number of new twists. It should be a double dam with 1000 feet of water between the crests. At each end there should be a wide gap, spanned by bridges of such a height that any ocean liner could pass under them. The canal between the dams would provide an avenue of quiet water for boat travel (freight) in any kind of weather; navigation would be perfectly safe even in the densest of fogs because the lights on the crowns of the dams would guide vessels. The dams themselves would carry railroad tracks and highways for cars and trucks, protected against storms by high and heavy stone walls. There would be no ventilation problems, —and the Royal Navy and Air Force could patrol every foot of the whole structure 24 hours a day.

The Second World War broke out a few years after the tunnel project had been rejected once more. And in December 1939, at a meeting of the Allied Supreme War Council, the tunnel problem came up promptly. Was there still time to build it? And what would it cost? The engineers could not answer the first question, but they had a ready reply for the second: 60 million pounds sterling. Since the defense budget of England and France together came to 6 million pounds a day it was easy to figure out that the tunnel would save money if it shortened the war by just two weeks. The German attack (and victory) in the West saved the Supreme War Council from having to make a decision. The British evacuated their army from Dunkirk by boat, losing few men but all their equipment. If they had had the tunnel they would have escaped with still fewer losses and most of their equipment.

Later in the war British airmen reported German building activity near Calais and Sangatte, and considerable apprehension was aroused. It would be entirely possible to dig the tunnel from one end only. The British put listening devices into their pilot tunnel so they could hear the Germans drilling, if they did. Actually they were building launching sites for V-1 flying bombs and V-2 long-range rockets. But the Germans also put listening devices into the French pilot tunnel just in case the English started drilling.

And the very end of the war saw something which was at least reminiscent of earlier Channel tunnel plans. Its name was "Operation Pluto," the name being derived from "*Pipe Lines Under*

5. A Conundrum being towed across the Channel, laying a pipeline. German planes watched the operation but what the Germans thought about it is still unknown.

The Ocean." It started in April 1942 when Admiral Lord Louis Mountbatten attended a demonstration of new flame-throwers. Geoffrey Lloyd, in charge of petroleum, who was present, asked whether there was anything else his department could do. "Yes," said the admiral. "Can you lay an oil pipeline across the Channel?"

Engineering firms were doubtful at first. Of course it might be done under peacetime conditions, but with German planes overhead, German naval units only a few score miles away, and possibly German submarines under the keel? But two develop-

ment groups said that they would at least try. One group was headed by engineer A. C. Hartley of the Anglo-Iranian Oil Company, who suggested making 3-inch pipes like the outer sheaths of submarine cables, leaving out the cores and insulation. The firm of Siemens & Henleys did the actual work, and the pipe was dubbed "Hais" (Hartley–Anglo-Iranian–Siemens) pipe. Most of the Hais pipe used was made in the United States, 140 miles of it. The other group consisted mainly of two engineers, H. A. Hammick and B. J. Ellis. Their pipe was called "Hamel" (from the two names), and 350 miles of it were made in England. Hammick and Ellis knew that 3-inch steel pipe could be wound on drums and be reasonably straight after unreeling, provided the drums were big enough. The drums used were enormous,

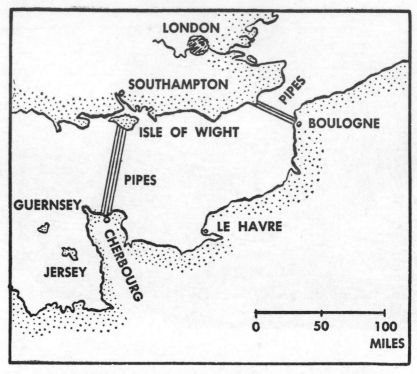

6. Operation Pluto, showing the location of the pipelines

90 feet long, with a diameter of 60 feet, and flanges 6 feet high. Empty, each drum weighed 270 tons; with 70 miles of pipe the weight was 1600 tons. These giant bobbins were called "Conundrums" and were also made in England. For laying the pipelines, each Conundrum (there were six in all) was towed by two tugs, while a third kept the whole on a straight course (see fig. 5).

The operations must have been watched by the Germans, who presumably were puzzled by the process. But for reasons of their own they never interfered. Operation Pluto put four pipelines across the Channel from the Isle of Wight to Cherbourg and sixteen from Dungeness to Boulogne. Between August 12,

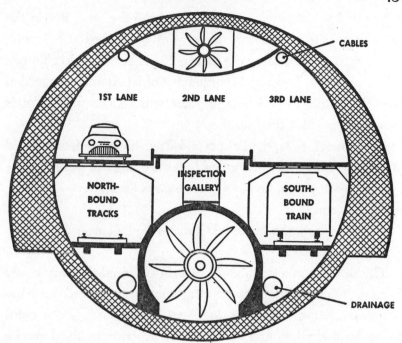

CABLES

1ST LANE 2ND LANE 3RD LANE

INSPECTION GALLERY

NORTH-BOUND TRACKS

SOUTH-BOUND TRAIN

DRAINAGE

7. Basdevant's tunnel for automobiles and railroad

1944, and May 8, 1945, 120 million gallons of gasoline were pumped through these pipes to fuel the Allied armies in Europe.

The two pilot tunnels are now being watched by one man each, one in England and one in France. They are as dry as they were when Queen Victoria was shown around. But in her day it had been planned as a railroad tunnel only, the engineers of the period after the second World War began thinking in terms of a combined railroad and vehicular tunnel. The design made by the French engineer André Basdevant (fig. 7) incorporated a three-lane highway.

In 1959 the Channel Tunnel story moved forward a little by virtue of the fact that test borings were made from shipboard across the channel to establish whether the layers of rock corresponded to the situation at both ends all the way. But in the same year British military men went on record once more, opposing the tunnel. However, the political climate had changed a little, for the Viscount Montgomery of El Alamain conceded that the public should have the last word, since public funds would be used for the building.

In February 1964, the British and French governments issued statements *that they had agreed to build a railroad tunnel under the Channel.* The 162-year argument was finally terminated by an agreement.

So we are going to have the Channel Tunnel after all.

Well, not yet.

The British spokesman said: "Bearing in mind the very heavy burden of the two countries' existing commitments and the many other competing claims on their national resources, it remains to be decided when and how best the expense involved can be sustained." The French spokesman said the same thing; that the French version sounded a little more optimistic might have been due to a somewhat different attitude, or just to the difference in language.

The expense involved is now estimated at $400 million and the construction time at five to six years. Private capital is willing to finance at least part of the expense, but both governments are hesitant on that point.

The progress made consists in ending the long period of opposition on principle. But everything else still has to come.

2. ISLANDS AFLOAT

Islands Afloat

Unlike the concept of the tunnel from England to France, which
has a history of one and a half centuries, the idea of a floating
platform in the middle of the ocean is only a few decades old,

8. An Armstrong seadrome on the high seas

for it originated at the time when mankind learned to fly and began dreaming about flying the ocean.

The first attempt at crossing the Atlantic Ocean by air was made quite early in the history of aviation by the American journalist Walter Wellman. Since the year was 1910, Wellman naturally did not try to do it with an airplane. He used a dirigible of an over-all length of 228 feet, which was named the *America* but had been built in France and had made its first transatlantic trip in the hold of a cargo steamer. The airship cast off from Atlantic City on October 15, 1910. Wellman and his men were fished out of the ocean some 375 miles east of Norfolk, Virginia. Although the attempt was a failure as far as crossing the ocean was concerned, the flight did produce a few "firsts." The total distance traveled was 1008 miles—no other dirigible had made so long a flight. And the radio distress call that Wellman had sent out was the first distress call from the air.

The first successful flights across the ocean occurred nine years later. On May 16, 1919, a Curtiss NC-4 flying boat took off from Trepassey Bay, Newfoundland. Piloted by Walter Hinton and commanded by Lieutenant Commander (later Rear Admiral) Albert Cushing Read, the flying boat reached Horta, Azores Islands, the next day and then proceeded at a more leisurely pace to Lisbon, Portugal, and from there to Plymouth, England. The total distance covered was 4514 miles. On June 14 of the same year Sir John Alcock and Sir Arthur Whitten-Brown flew a Vickers-Vimy biplane from St. Johns, Newfoundland, to Clifden, Ireland. And just two weeks later the British airship R-34 crossed the ocean in the opposite direction. Commanded by Major G. H. Scott and carrying thirty-one people— including one American observer and one English stowaway— the R-34 flew from the Firth of Forth in Scotland to Roosevelt Field, near Mineola, Long Island, in 108 hours. The return flight took only 75 hours.

Thus by the middle of 1919 the North Atlantic Ocean had

been crossed by air in both directions.[1] The South Atlantic did not have to wait long. On May 31, 1922, two Portuguese pilots, Vice-Admiral Gago Coutinho and Captain Sacadura Cabral, flew a Fairey seaplane from Lisbon to Las Palmas, Canary Islands, from there to the Cape Verde Islands, and then to St. Paul's Rock, an island off the coast of Brazil.

All this proved that ocean flying could be done. But it wasn't easy. And even if it had been easier it wasn't profitable. Ocean flying came under the heading of sports, not transportation. And along the most important transatlantic traffic lane—from the English Channel to New York—there is nothing but water. If only there were a few nice islands for intermediate stops!

At that point somebody thought of a solution: why not *build* such islands? Not real islands, of course. That was impossible, since the depth of the ocean on that route is never less than a mile and usually about 2 miles. But floating islands, floating airports where a plane could land and replenish its fuel tanks or outwait a period of bad weather, might be another story.

Partly because most ocean flights so far had been made by flying boats or pontoon-equipped seaplanes, partly because the firm of Dornier had just started building a series of very successful flying boats of various sizes, but mostly because this was after all ocean flying, the first design for such a floating airport was tailored to fit the needs of flying boats.

[1] Charles A. Lindbergh's flight across the Atlantic was not the first, as many people seem to believe. His flight, on May 20, 1927, from Roosevelt Field to Le Bourget, Paris, was the first nonstop transatlantic flight from the North American continent to the continent of Europe. It was also the first solo flight. But Captain Clarence D. Chamberlin followed close on Lindbergh's heels when he flew from Roosevelt Field to Eisleben, Germany, June 4–6, 1927. He carried a passenger but no co-pilot.

The first design had the shape of a horseshoe, measuring about 900 feet in length and almost that much across at the widest part. It was to be built of steel girders, with a double skin of thin steel plate. Naturally it was to be compartmented inside so that a leak would not endanger the whole; it would have stayed afloat even if half of its compartments were filled with water, provided that they were not all on the same side of the horseshoe. The structure was to be secured in position by so-called sea anchors reaching down into layers of the ocean where there are neither waves nor currents. In this way it would always head into the wind, with the two "legs" of the horseshoe pointing away from the direction from which the wind was blowing. The space between the legs would provide a large, quiet lagoon for flying boats and pontoon planes. The legs would be runways for small land-based aircraft. There would be a repair shop, a few hangars, a radio station, a hotel, and even two ocean-going tugs to tow in any flying boats that might make emergency landings some distance away.

The plans made exciting pictures for the illustrated magazines, but while there was no doubt about the usefulness of such a structure, marine engineers began to wonder about the problem of building one. The whole structure would be subjected to a little wave action all the time and to quite violent wave action some of the time. To withstand that it should be both rigid and flexible, a problem that also comes up in the design of large ocean liners. But while the engineers did have experience with long ocean liners they had none with a structure of such an unusual shape.

Possibly the most unfortunate aspect of the whole project was that one floating airport would not be enough. In order to cut the total distance into hops that would be easy for the airplanes of that time, at least four seadromes would be needed. After some discussion the idea was quietly filed away, pending improved aircraft on the one hand and improved airport design on the other.

An alternate design, advanced when the engineers confessed their lack of experience with a structure of such shape, tried to replace the horseshoe by an arrow in a circle. The reasoning was that one could have a seadrome and a quiet lagoon without having the seadrome itself produce the quiet lagoon. In this design the seadrome proper was a flat-topped ship's hull—an aircraft carrier, we would call it now. The ship's hull was to be held in position by a sea anchor and would always—it was hoped—turn into the wind. The quiet lagoon was to be created by a 3000-foot circle of concrete pontoons which would stop the wave action. The main questions were whether the circle of concrete pontoons would remain a circle, and how to keep the flattop in the approximate center of the lagoon.

There followed a silence of about 5 years, during which period aircraft grew better and better, and the trend in design was definitely away from flying boats and pontoon planes and in the direction of land-based long-range airplanes. This trend was clearly reflected in the design of a floating airport published in 1928–29, which was meant for land-based aircraft only.

This was the "Armstrong seadrome," named after its designer, the American engineer Edward R. Armstrong. It immediately aroused widespread interest and approval. Louis Blériot, who first flew the English Channel, in a plane of his own design, expressed himself as being enthusiastically in favor of floating seadromes and especially of Armstrong's design. During an in-

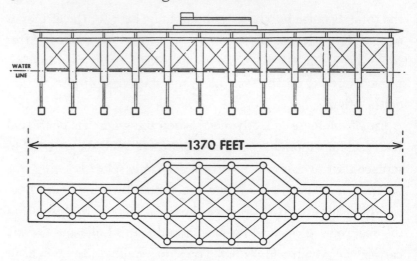

9. The first Armstrong seadrome: side view (above), and plan (below)

terview in 1934 he said, "It is commonly assumed that the idea of floating airports in mid-ocean has been discarded. On the contrary, they have never been more necessary for transatlantic air service. . . . Seadromes are not designed to make regular transatlantic flights possible, but to make them profitable." President Franklin D. Roosevelt also said on more than one occasion that he was attracted by Armstrong's proposal.

Armstrong's seadrome, very carefully engineered from the flight deck to the sea anchor, was essentially a large rectangular platform, 1370 feet long and over 350 feet wide, raised 100 feet above the surface of the ocean, 60 feet higher than the highest ocean waves ever recorded. Of course the platform was not to be just a flat sheet of metal; it rather corresponded to a deck on an ocean liner. Underneath the flight deck there would be storage rooms and machine shops, kitchens and laundries, dining and recreation rooms, crew quarters and staterooms, probably also a laboratory for marine biology and, of course, a weather station—in short, a complete airport with a hotel thrown in.

The platform was to stand on thirty-two tall legs, called pylons, which reached down into the water and widened out into buoyant chambers below the level of wave action. The buoyant chambers were to be accessible through the pylons for inspection and some of them might be used for storage purposes, especially for liquids such as fresh water, oil, and Diesel fuel for the floating airport's power plant. Unlike a ship, the floating airport would be perfectly stable even in the worst weather. The waves would pass through under the deck between the pylons.

It is important to realize at this point that a wave does not behave the way it looks to the eye. The over all appearance of a wave is that of a hill of water moving broadside-on over the surface of the ocean. But at any point along the course of the wave the performance of the individual water particles is little more than a simple up-and-down movement. This fact can easily be tested by throwing something that will float in the path of an oncoming wave (some distance from the shore). The piece of wood or cork will be lifted by the wave and then sink into the trough without being moved laterally to any great extent. A ship's hull, being a solid wall, will be battered by the waves which are obstructed by it; a set of piles in deep water will at most cause some minor splashing. Armstrong's seadrome, by its very design, successfully avoided the most criticized defect of the floating horseshoe; it would not impede wave action and therefore would not suffer from it.

And while the flight deck might be windswept in bad weather

it would not even get wet, unless rain happened to be falling. The floating airport was to be indirectly anchored to the bottom of the sea. The anchor, which was carefully designed, was to be of the type called a mushroom anchor, but enormous in size. It was to be buoyant enough to float at first, for towing into position, with chambers holding the wire rope. When the proper spot was reached, the buoyancy chambers of the anchor would be flooded in succession, while the wire rope was simultaneously payed out. When the anchor finally rested on the bottom, digging its way into the ooze by its weight, the wire rope was to lead up to the surface and the seadrome, but not directly. Almost vertically above the anchor there was to be a structure similar in design to the seadrome, but much smaller. This "rope buoy" would be used as a surface anchor for the seadrome.

Armstrong's project, received with much enthusiasm by professionals, made rapid progress at first. A scale model ($\frac{1}{32}$-inch to 1 inch) was built and much photographed. A few sections were built on a larger scale and tested. But after an initial fast start things just slowed down, as they often do. The slow but sure approach of the Second World War was probably one of the deterrent factors. But when the war broke out in Europe, thinking about the seadromes suddenly began to resemble the thinking about the Channel Tunnel on the other side of the Atlantic Ocean. Not that anybody in America ever seriously denounced seadromes as "stepping stones" for a possible invader, but military men in the United States and in Canada began to consider how useful they would be if they existed. At that time all the bombers sent to Great Britain could be flown across directly, and many were, but fighter aircraft had to be carried on shipboard. With three seadromes—the number usu-

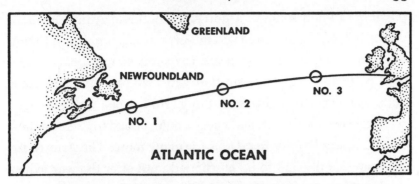

10. Location of the three seadromes for transatlantic flying

ally advocated—in existence, the fighters could have made the trip by air. The bombers could have carried war materials as payload. Most important, the seadromes themselves could have been fighter bases to protect American surface convoys from the enemy's long-range aircraft, and especially from his submarines.

The vulnerability of the seadromes would have been low. Their fighter squadrons could have defended them against air assault. Guns could have been mounted on them (imagine having a steady firing platform at sea!) for defense against both air attack and attack by smaller surface craft. Even submarines would have had a tough time disposing of an Armstrong seadrome. Since the pylons are spaced more than 100 feet apart a torpedo could not be expected to destroy more than one buoyant chamber and pylon. And a seadrome could afford to lose half a dozen without any worse effects than dipping a few feet deeper into the water. To sink a seadrome a submarine would have to torpedo at least ten pylons, all on one side!

While it was generally admitted that seadromes would have been useful to have, it was also generally realized that it was impossible to build some in a hurry. To build an Armstrong sea-drome takes time, and time was merely one of a number of things that were lacking. American industry was simply busy. Every steel plate and every I-beam that was being rolled in the steel mills was earmarked for something. And every welder, every riveter, every machinist, and every engineer had his defense job, and there would have been jobs for many more. The Armstrong seadrome simply had to be postponed until after the war, when steel and the men to work it would be available.

But might it not be possible to build something resembling a seadrome, serviceable for military purposes but simpler in con-struction? Something that did not use materials short in supply and which did not require skilled labor? That such an *ersatz* seadrome, somewhat makeshift and clumsy but useful just the same, was possible was argued by an officer of the Coast Artillery Reserve named Charles F. McReynolds.

He suggested an enormous compartmented "brick" of con-crete, 1500 feet long, 500 feet wide, and 120 feet thick, with 10-foot-thick outer walls. Inside it was to be divided into 750 water-tight cubbyholes (each considerably bigger than a large living room) by means of reinforced concrete walls 1 foot thick. In spite of its enormous weight, the "brick" would float with its top side 40 feet above water level; 80 feet of its mass would be submerged and 30 feet of that would be below the level of wave action in quiet water. An elevation of 40 feet above sea level would be enough except for the most unusual kind of weather. The average storm wave in the Atlantic Ocean is only 8 feet high and the "length" of these waves—the distance from one wave-crest to the next—is about 200 feet. The highest waves ever re-corded were 40 feet high from crest to trough, but this means that the wave action extends 20 feet in both directions from the normal water level, so that even such very unusual waves would not reach to the top of the "brick."

That one can build floating structures of concrete is no novelty; not only are there bridges which rest on concrete floats, but thousands of concrete barges and ships are in use daily. Whether McReynolds' "brick" could have been towed into position is a more pertinent question.

Probably the largest structure towed so far over open ocean was a floating drydock which was 860 feet long and over 165 feet wide. Experience with the towing of this and other large drydocks has shown that it can be done, provided you don't insist on speed. In fact, it takes surprisingly little power to tow something *slowly*. In the 1930s large log rafts were towed along the Pacific Coast from Seattle to San Diego. These rafts, held together in a primitive manner by chains, had a draft comparable to that of the biggest ocean liners, namely 28 feet. They were over 1000 feet long, about 60 feet wide, and weighed more than 15,000 tons. They were towed by *one* tugboat with a 1000-horsepower engine! And this was not done just once, in exceptionally fine weather, but 118 times, in any kind of weather. Of the 118 rafts that left Seattle, 115 reached San Diego. Two broke up en route, and one, incredible as it may seem, caught fire.

The reason that a single 1000-horsepower tug could move those huge log rafts is, to repeat, that nobody insisted on high speed. The speed at which they were actually towed was equal to that of a man walking briskly. For such low speeds, and up to twice the speed of a walking man, the speed/power relationship is simple: the power requirement increases with the square of the speed. In other words, if 1000 horsepower will tow something at 3 miles per hour, you need 4000 horsepower to tow it at 6 miles per hour. But once the speed passes 10 miles per hour the power requirements go up in a fantastic manner. The British battleship *Royal Oak* required 40,000 horsepower to make 22 knots, the *Rodney* needed 45,000 horsepower to make 23 knots, the *Queen Elizabeth* has 80,000 horsepower and does 24 knots, the battle cruiser *Hood* had 144,000 horsepower to do 31 knots, and the aircraft carrier *Lexington* developed 210,000 horsepower for a 34.5-knot record run. But it was calculated that the *Lexington* could have moved with a speed of 5 knots (or just about 6 miles per hour) on a mere 100 horsepower.

The knowledge of such figures is important to such problems as towing a seadrome into position. It is also important with respect to the anchoring of a seadrome. Since the seadrome is not influenced by wave action it can be moved from its assigned position only by ocean currents, of which the Gulf Stream is the best-known example. The speed of such currents in the open Atlantic is never more than 1½ miles per hour. If the wind happens to blow in the same direction as the current flows a seadrome might be moved at the rate of 5 miles per hour, but such "fast" movement would be rather exceptional. Even this highest speed would be counteracted by the power of one tug with a 1000-horsepower engine, or 1500 horsepower if you want to be absolutely sure. It is possible, therefore, that the heavy sea anchor and the separate structure of the "line buoy" are not necessary at all and that it might be cheaper and simpler to equip the floating airport with slight motive power—or just to keep an ocean-going tug handy.

The large concrete "brick" advocated by McReynolds was not built; the idea was even released for publication during the war.

But there was another floating island project which was kept secret so well that its release after the war created a big surprise all around, especially in circles of naval officers. This was Project Habakkuk. The reason for the name can be found in the Bible; Habakkuk was the prophet who said, "I will work a work in your days which ye will not believe, though it be told you." Well, it wasn't told until afterward, but people might well have disbelieved it even if it had been told.

The idea originated with Geoffrey Pyke, who was on Lord Mountbatten's staff, in about 1942. He suggested, primarily as an antisubmarine measure, an "unsinkable aircraft carrier"—an artificial iceberg. "H.M.S. Habakkuk," the iceberg-carrier, was to have the general shape of a ship, 2000 feet long, 300 feet wide, and 200 feet deep. Enough motive power to move it into place and prevent its drifting was to be provided by means of a number of propellers, mounted on engine nacelles. Its weight would have been 2 million tons.

Any iceberg, natural or otherwise, will slowly melt away if exposed to warm water. If H.M.S. Habakkuk had been just a million tons of ice stationed somewhere around the British Isles it might have stood up through 3 months of winter but would not have lasted far into April. However, not much power is needed to keep a large chunk of ice frozen. Consequently Habakkuk was to be equipped with refrigeration coils in the outer layers of its girth and bottom; if the outside could be kept frozen the interior would not melt.

When Geoffrey Pyke presented his idea to Lord Mountbatten, the latter was impressed by it and passed it on to the Chiefs of Staff. The Chiefs of Staff forwarded it to the War Cabinet and from there it went to the British Prime Minister, Winston

11. "H.M.S. Habakkuk," the iceberg-carrier

Churchill. It captured Churchill's imagination and he endorsed it with the words, "Let us cut a large chunk of ice from the Arctic icecap and tow it down past Cornwall, fly on our aircraft and tow it to the point of attack." The actual work, for climatic as well as for security reasons, was to be done in Canada. A block model 60 feet long, 30 feet wide, and 20 feet deep, weighing 1000 tons, was built at Patricia Lake near Jasper, Canada. This block model was kept frozen from the winter 1942–43 until the end of the summer of 1943.

Although it is almost impossible to ruin a natural iceberg by gunfire—it has been tried often, sometimes just for target practice—the engineers in charge felt that pure ice was too brittle and might crack. Obviously the ice had to be reinforced in some manner. This was done by mixing wood pulp, the raw material of paper, with the water before freezing it. The amount of wood pulp used ranged between 4 and 14 per cent of the total water volume. When water mixed with wood pulp froze, a new substance resulted which received the name of "pykrete." It was a tough unbrittle solid, slightly plastic, which could be sawed like wood. It was also very resistant to shock. An ordinary block of ice can be split by a smart stroke of a heavy chopper. From a block of pykrete the chopper's blade bounced off. A revolver bullet bounced off likewise, though a bullet from the same revolver shattered a block of clear ice. On the basis of these tests it was estimated that a full-size submarine torpedo exploding against the pykrete side of Habakkuk would produce nothing worse than a crater 3 feet deep and not much bigger across.

If a block of pykrete was dropped into fairly warm water the wood-pulp fibers, sticking out from the surface where some of the ice had melted off, formed an insulating layer which considerably retarded further melting. Even though the engineers ran into a number of unforeseen difficulties, the scheme could probably have been made to work eventually. But other antisubmarine measures had been so successful in the meantime that there was no need to go on with Project Habakkuk, which, as Winston Churchill expressed it, "was reluctantly dropped" by the end of 1943.

But what about the Armstrong seadrome?

During the same year in which the block model of Habakkuk

was finally permitted to melt, it was announced that Pennsylvania Central Airlines had filed an application with the Civil Aeronautics Board for the construction and operation of three Armstrong seadromes between New York and England. Since the airline distance from New York to London is 3680 miles, each hop, if the seadromes were spaced equally, would be just 920 miles.

Along with this announcement Armstrong published his new design. It was the same in all essentials as the first, but as to details there were a large number of modernizing touches. As a whole the new design provided for a longer seadrome, 3550 feet, with a maximum width of 400 feet. The runway in the center of the flight deck was to be 150 feet wide. There was to be less superstructure. The pylons had been improved too; they were to be telescoping for towing into position and had ballast chambers that would reach far down into the sea when the pylon was fully extended. Some of them also carried engines and propellers to lessen the strain on the mooring cable in high winds. The flight deck was not to be floodlighted at night, which might temporarily blind a pilot; instead, landing lights under heavy glass cover were to be imbedded in the flight deck itself.

The cost of such an improved seadrome was estimated at 10 million dollars, and it was stated that the three seadromes planned for the transatlantic air route would be built as soon as steel (and steelworkers) became available after the war.

But then nothing happened.

The reason was that airplanes had in the meantime outgrown the need for seadromes. Offhand it may seem as if a seadrome would still increase the capacity of an airplane to carry payload, since it obviously needs to carry less fuel for a 1000-mile flight than for a 3000-mile flight nonstop. But there are more factors involved than simply the distance to be flown. You could not let a plane take off, say, in New York, with just enough fuel to reach seadrome no. 1. During the 3 hours the flight would take the weather could change completely. Seadrome no. 1 might be enshrouded in a dense fog, especially since no. 1 would be not far from Newfoundland, an area where dense fogs occur often during certain seasons.

Since radar guidance was not then developed for commercial flying, the airliner would have had to carry enough fuel either to return to the airport from which it took off or to another airport on the mainland, or to disregard seadrome no. 1 which is "closed in" (as they say in airplane parlance) and proceed to seadrome no. 2. But since any airplane has to carry a fuel reserve for an extra 1000 miles for simple safety reasons the gain in payload-carrying capacity becomes fairly small.

Modern airliners fly the Atlantic Ocean directly from New York most of the time. An alternative route is to go to Newfoundland from New York and cut across from there. Now the nonstop distance from Newfoundland to Paris is very nearly the same as the nonstop distance from Los Angeles to New York. We can therefore draw comparisons from actual flying practice; the nonstop flight from Los Angeles to New York can be compared to the ocean flight, while the Los Angeles–New York flight with stops at intermediate cities can be compared to an ocean flight with seadromes.

A Constellation making the transcontinental flight directly— distance about 2450 miles—has to carry 18,800 pounds of gasoline [2] and has an available payload capacity of 13,750 pounds. If

[2] Amounting to 3133 gallons.

all seats are sold, it carries fifty-seven passengers, and since the airlines consider every passenger, young or old, stout or slender, as weighing 195 pounds, this accounts for a theoretical 11,115 pounds, leaving 2635 pounds for what is called "open weight."

The same flight is made by the same type of Constellation with intermediate landings in Kansas City and in Chicago. The mileages flown are: Los Angeles to Kansas City, 1368 miles; Kansas City to Chicago, 420 miles; Chicago to New York, 724 miles; making a total of 2512 miles. (Actually of course the total mileage is somewhat more because of traffic patterns in and out of airports and occasional waits in the air, spent circling around until everything is clear for a landing.) The fuel carried between stops is actually less, 11,400 pounds, 4000 pounds, and 6200 pounds,[3] but for practical operations the payload stays the same —13,750 pounds.

Applied to ocean flying this means that, assuming the existence of three seadromes, one can increase the payload by a fair percentage on paper but would not dare to do so in reality— certainly not to an extent which would pay for the seadromes. Whether a seadrome would pay if operated essentially as a novel kind of resort hotel with some incidental airline patronage is a different question which nobody can answer fully.

But in a modified form the Armstrong seadrome may still become a reality. In 1949 the Coast Guard approached Armstrong with a request for a design of a small seadrome for a special purpose. In the course of its duties the Coast Guard operates something like meteorological stations on the high seas, using its regu-

[3] Respectively, 1900, 667, and 1033 gallons, making a total of 3600 gallons, or 21,600 pounds. The figures for jets are different, but bear the same relationship to each other.

lar vessels. To maintain one such "station" the Coast Guard needs three vessels, cruising in relays. Each of the three vessels has a crew of 120 officers and men. A small seadrome, anchored in the proper place, could do the same job as the three vessels, with some additional assignments thrown in, and would need a crew of only 80 officers and men. Armstrong responded to the Coast Guard's request with a design for a diamond-shaped seadrome, with a flight deck for helicopters only, resting on five pylons.

Such a small seadrome might still materialize. But the big ones probably will not, because aviation, which they were to serve, was impatient enough to fly away from them.

3. THE TAMED VOLCANO

12. The volcanic power plant at Larderello, Italy

The Tamed Volcano

There is an island in the Atlantic Ocean which is only a little smaller than Cuba; it has an area of not quite 40,000 square miles while Cuba comprises a little more than 44,000 square miles. This island can also be described as somewhat larger than Ireland, which consists of slightly less than 32,000 square miles. But while Cuba and Ireland support populations of more than 4 million people apiece, this island feeds only 120,000 inhabitants, because three-quarters of its area are uninhabitable and even the remaining quarter is thinly settled.

In late summer of 1952 the government of the island—one of the oldest democracies on the globe—decided to make a present to the native children. Each boy and girl under six years of age was given five bananas which had just been harvested.

The name of that island?

Unless you know the answer you could never guess, in spite of, or rather because of, the five freshly harvested bananas given to each child. It is Iceland.

Iceland lies high up in the cold North Atlantic, its northernmost peninsula actually touching the Arctic Circle. And Iceland is the island of enormous and permanent snowfields: Myrdals-jökull and Langjökull, Hofsjökull and Vatnajökull; the last, which is the largest, with an area of 3280 square miles, about three times as large as the whole state of Rhode Island.

How can they harvest bananas in Iceland?

They can because Iceland is not only the island of large snow-fields and glaciers, it is also the island of active volcanoes and hot springs. Always remember that the one Icelandic word which has become international is *geysir*, even though it is somewhat mistakenly used in the other languages which have adopted it. In Iceland *geysir* is the name of a specific geyser which is usually called the Great Geyser; the general term for a hot spring is *hver*. Geographers for centuries have referred to Iceland as the "island of fire and ice." A story has it that the Viking Ingolfr Arnarsson named the bay in which he arrived Reykjavik, or "Smoky Bay," because all around the mountains smoked, and steam rose from the ground, something he had never seen in his native Norway. The bay has changed names since then and is now called Faxafjördr (or Faxa Bay), but Ingolfr Arnarsson's term has remained too, as the name of the island's capital.

Iceland is completely volcanic. Its mountains are either dead volcanoes or active ones; its plains are frozen lava flows. And where there is volcanism, past or present, there are hot springs; Iceland has about fifteen hundred of them.

Naturally the inhabitants of Iceland have made some restricted use of the hot springs ever since the island was settled. It is easier by far to wash pots and pans and clothing in hot water than in cold. Icelandic women took advantage of this fact if a nonviolent hot spring was handy. In New Zealand, where hot springs are abundant too, Maori maidens still do the same thing every day, and presumably our Indians once did the same in the area which is now Yellowstone National Park.

But washing pots and clothing in a hot spring that happens to be on the property, and really utilizing a hot spring, are two different things. As short a time ago as 1910 no Icelander had any conception of what his island's hot springs could do for him. Nor did anybody else.

It was in 1915 or 1916 that a Hungarian scientist, Dr. Szilard Zielinsky, then professor of engineering at the Engineering College of Budapest, first evolved a plan. A hot spring, Professor Zielinsky reasoned, has to force its way to the surface through rocks and around obstacles. This often causes the flow to be irregular. But if one opened up a nice smooth well for such a spring one could count on a steady supply of hot water. In short, one could drill for hot water if the locality were right, just as one drills for cold water elsewhere or for oil if there is any in the ground. And even if the naturally hot water should prove useless for bathing or cooking because of chemicals dissolved in it, it could still be sent through radiators to heat homes and factories.

After explaining just what could be done if so and so many gallons of scalding water could be captured every second, and how much coal could be saved per gallon per second, Professor Zielinsky pointed out that there were hot springs near Budapest. They would not heat the whole city in winter because the springs were too small—or the city too big—but they would save so and so many tons of coal every year.

Since this was during the First World War one would think that the city council and the government would have jumped at the opportunity. They didn't. They said that it could not be done in time of war for lack of materials and manpower. And they added that it was not even a postwar project, for it couldn't be done in time of peace either. One could not drill a hot well. And even if it were possible to drill a hot well the hot water could not be conducted through pipes and still be hot water at the other end of the pipeline.

Budapest is still without volcanic heat. But Iceland has it.

The Icelanders began in 1930, at first on a small scale, of course. The first hot-water wells were drilled in the Reykir Valley, about 10 miles from Reykjavik. It must be said that the Icelanders were lucky. Their natural hot water could have been fouled with sulfur compounds or muddied with sediments carried in suspension by the water. As it happens, the Icelandic hot water is virtually free of chemical impurities and carries so little sediment that it can be used directly in swimming pools—with the addition of a fair amount of cold water, for it is 190 degrees Fahrenheit when it comes out of the ground. The first buildings in Reykjavik to be heated with hot water from the Reykir Valley were the State Hospital, two public schools, and fifty-six private homes. By 1935 the Icelanders, under the guidance of Chief Engineer Björnsson, had drilled fourteen hot wells, with a total production of 1500 gallons of near-boiling water every minute.

In 1951 the number of hot wells had increased to forty-three, and all public buildings and 75 per cent of all private homes in Reykjavik were heated by them. And not only heated, because the hot water is also used directly from hot-water taps.

The whole procedure now closely resembles the hot-water supply for an apartment building, enlarged to serve a whole city, and with the difference that the "furnace" is subterranean heat. At the pumping stations the water first runs through filters

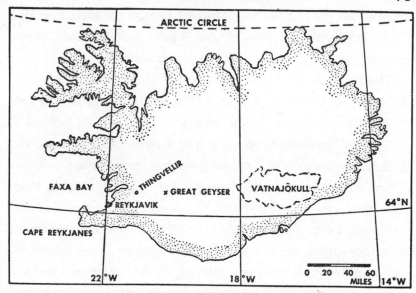

13. Iceland

to remove the little sediment there is. After passing the filters it travels for 10 miles overland in concrete conduits, with only a negligible loss of heat. Near the city it is stored in seven enormous containers, each capable of holding 35,000 cubic feet of hot water. Distribution is from there, and the home-owner Vilhjalmur Thorgilsson, just like his neighbor Gudmundur Gunnarsson, receives his heat as a utility like electric current and pays for it—one hopes—within 10 days after receipt of the monthly bill.

Production is now 45,000 gallons per minute or slightly over 1 million cubic feet per 24-hour period. In July the city of Reykjavik needs only about 350,000 cubic feet daily, but in January and February it needs over 800,000 cubic feet.

In addition to providing for the city, the hot water also heats the greenhouses where food-producing plants of the temperate zone and of the subtropics are grown. In 1952 the total floor area of these greenhouses was 750,000 square feet, but this area is growing steadily, almost like the plants inside.

The Icelanders are convinced that all this is just a beginning. The next step will be to tap really deep and really hot pockets of their volcanic foundation, which will yield steam instead of hot water. The steam then will run steam turbine generators, and Iceland's volcanism will produce electric current too.

But when they do find steam pockets, as they must in time, and build such a power plant, the design engineer will not be confronted with an entirely new set of problems. He won't have to gather experience in a novel field as he goes along. In fact, he will be able to call in for consultation fellow engineers who have such experience. Or, if he prefers, he can board an airliner and fly to inspect an actual volcanic power plant which has been operating for half a century.

It is located in Italy, in the district which the Italians call Toscana and we call Tuscany, on the west side of the Italian peninsula, bordering the Ligurian Sea. The actual site of that volcanic power plant is not associated with any famous city, but near it is a whole collection of famous places and cities. Just off-shore is the island of Elba, where Napoleon was imprisoned. To the north of the volcanic region is the district of Chianti which gave its name to the famous wine; north of that district is Florence (Firenze), the city of the Medici. There is Pisa of leaning-tower fame, where Galileo Galilei taught. And even closer to the volcanic region is Siena, which gave its name to a whole school of painting.

The power plant itself is at a place named Larderello, 12½ miles due south of Volterra. Many square miles in this section

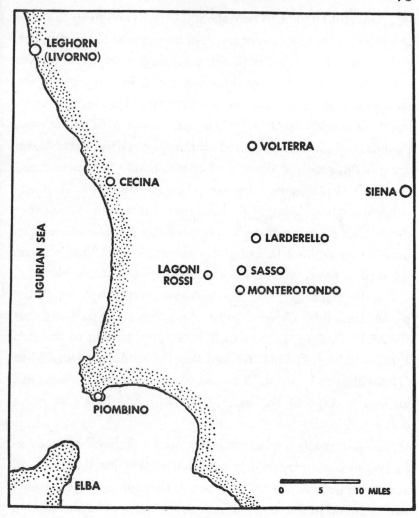

14. Tuscany

of Tuscany consist of landscapes that look as if they were not on our planet at all. The soil is baked to a dry reddish-yellow color by the subterranean heat. It is even hot to the touch. There is a constant smell of sulfur and of hydrogen sulfide in the air, not powerful enough to be unbearable but enough so that one is always aware of its presence. And from cracks in the dry, hot, red soil steam escapes with a loud hissing noise. The natives call these steam vents *soffioni* or *fumacchi*. In many places the steam does not blow into the air directly but issues into small basins of muddy water which is hot, smelly with sulfur compounds, and violently agitated all the time. These water basins are called *lagoni* and there is, of course, no life in or near them. But in a few places near dry steam vents or *soffioni* freakish circumstances have brought it about that a part of the steam condenses and moistens the ground while the main mass escapes into the air without touching the surroundings. There you can see well-watered green bushes under the white steam plume.

But this is a rarity; the general over-all impression recalls the phrase coined by General Sully when, in his campaign against the Sioux Indians, he had to fight an engagement in the Bad Lands of North Dakota. He said that the landscape looked like "Hell with the fires out." The area around Larderello looks like an earlier stage of the same: Hell with the fires just going out.

Naturally such a phenomenon could not have been overlooked in a country which has been settled for thousands of years as Italy has. The first mention of the *soffioni* and the *lagoni* can be found in the long Latin poem *De rerum Natura*, written by Titus Lucretius Carus, who died in 55 B.C. During the early Middle Ages the *soffioni* were mentioned in various documents and during the fourteenth century two learned men, both physicians, traveled to Tuscany to see them for themselves. One was Ugolino de Montecatini and the other was Andrea Bacci Elpidiani, head physician of the papal court. About a century later the great Georg Bauer, who called himself Georgius Agricola, added some more information about these phenomena.

There is some practical importance attached to the fact that the Tuscan *soffioni* have been described by somebody in every century. It proves that they have been active without interruption since the time of Christ or longer; one may safely conclude, therefore, that they will last for a few more centuries to come.

But up to the middle of the eighteenth century the volcanic manifestations of Tuscany had been treated mostly as a curiosity. They were something worth seeing and describing; they furnished material for a philosophical discourse or for a sermon. There was no thought of practical value in the minds of the savants who wrote about them. Nor did the local inhabitants put them to use as the Icelanders did. There was a good reason, however, for the water of the *lagoni,* while hot, is so dirty that things washed in it would hardly come out clean. The only people who found any use for the *lagoni* at all were a few coopers in the neighborhood who utilized some of the quieter basins for bending the staves they were making.

Things began to change near the end of the eighteenth century. One Dr. Giovanni Targioni-Tozzetti, also a physician, journeyed to Tuscany and studied the *soffioni.* But he did not look at the steam vents only; he was the first to publish a study of the geology of the area. His book appeared in Florence in 1769 and attracted the attention of one Hubertus Franz Hoefer, originally a German from Cologne on the Rhine, who, with his given names changed to Uberto Francesco, served as head pharmacist at the court of the Grand Duke of Tuscany. In 1777 Hoefer went to the small village of Monterotondo near which a fairly large *lagone* was known to exist. This one even had a name, being called Lagone Cerchiaio, in reference to the activity of the coopers.

Hoefer was certainly not the first man to taste the water of the *lagone* but he was the first to whom the taste meant anything. He recognized, in spite of mud and sulfur smells, that the water contained a substance he had in a glass jar in his pharmacy. We call it boric acid [1] but Hoefer had a different name for it. Precisely 75 years earlier, in 1702, the substance had been prepared for the first time by the Dutch naturalist Willem Homberg. It was therefore known as *sal sedativum Hombergi* or "Homberg's sedative salt."

Quite a stir was created by Hoefer's statement that this salt could be found "in the open" in the area which not only had seemed useless but had also been regarded with a great deal of superstition. A man whose proper scientific discipline was quite remote from either volcanism or chemistry—an anatomist whose name was Paolo Mascagni—hurried to the *lagoni* to check on the discovery. He found it to be correct and, being an eminently practical man, he at once began a series of studies on how the boric acid might be extracted from the water. At first as much of the water as possible had to be evaporated, naturally by means of heat. Well, there was heat enough around. Mascagni began to think of ways and means to use the volcanic heat to evaporate the volcanic water.

As soon as his studies were published, which was in 1779, several small companies began to acquire land in the region of the *soffioni* and *lagoni* in order to tap the natural source of *sal sedativum Hombergi*. The Tuscan boric-acid production was off to

[1] Or "boracic acid," a compound of boron with hydrogen and oxygen, with the formula H_3BO_3.

a start, with competition among the producers. Brouzet & Guerazzi competed with Chemin Pratt, who competed with La Motte, and all of them competed with a company from Leghorn (Livorno) by the name of Larderel & Co. The company from Leghorn won out and by 1818 it had absorbed all its competitors.

The method of evaporation used was developed by Signor Francesco de Larderel, the head of the firm. Artificial *lagoni* were built and were covered with brick hoods. They were almost

15. The trademark of the Larderello Company

round, but not quite; the largest had a major diameter of 65 feet and a minor diameter of 50 feet, the smallest measured 16 and 13 feet. The shape of these covered pools was so characteristic that the firm later used it as its trademark (fig. 15). Inside the brick dome the water from one of the nearby *lagoni* was held in a leaden pan which was then heated by natural steam. If possible the dome was built directly over a natural steam jet. If that could not be done it was built as near to a steam vent as feasible and the steam was led into the dome by means of clay pipes.

In 1842 the domes became obsolete because the new head of the firm, Adriano de Larderel, invented what became known as the "Adrian boiler," some of which are still in use. It consists of a shallow masonry trough, lined with lead, and about 230 feet long, with a width of 6 to 7 feet. The whole trough is built with a very gentle incline, about 1 foot per 100 feet of length, so that the "high" end of the trough is 2 feet and a few inches higher than the "low" end. Water will flow from one end to the other, but slowly. The speed is reduced even more by wooden slats nailed to the bottom of the trough about 2 feet apart. The water is of course introduced at the high end of the trough; the steam, flowing in the opposite direction, is introduced under the low end. Being heated through the lead, the water evaporates during its journey, and the amount introduced at the upper end is carefully calculated to produce the most concentrated solution of boric acid possible. This solution collects in basins at the low end of the trough and is then taken to the refinery.

In spite of all the intense activity the place did not have a name of its own for almost half a century; it had to be referred to with such circumlocutions as "the boric-acid factory near Montecerboli." Then Grand Duke Leopold II of Tuscany felt that the enterprise was important (and lucrative) enough to have a name of its own and on May 4, 1846, issued a proclamation christening the place Larderello.

Quite early Francesco de Larderel had conceived the idea that one might make a steam vent where Nature had failed to provide one, by drilling for steam. He tried it for the first time in 1832, with the type of drills used to drill for water. It did not work; we now know that such drills simply did not go deep enough. But the Larderels were not people who give up easily. Francesco continued to try, and Adriano after him. In 1856 they were finally successful, and the first artificial steam vent spouted a white plume high into the air.

The purpose of the drilling was still to obtain heat for industrial purposes, not to develop power. In fact, when visitors looking at the steam vents began to talk about the possibility of feeding the steam into a steam engine, they were usually told that they were—well, visitors, meaning outsiders, who did not understand this business any too well. If one tried to make this steam do work, it was explained, one would probably "kill" the steam vent. If it were fed into a steam engine the steam would meet resistance, and that would cause it to find different channels. Somewhere in the ground, it was reasoned, it would branch off to a new direction, finding a place somewhere where the resistance was less than in the steam engine.

Although Dr. Ferdinando Raynaut accepted this line of reasoning—we now know that it just isn't so—he still thought that the steam could be made to do work. Perhaps it was wrong to confine it too strongly, but it was still hot. So Dr. Raynaut took a multiple boiler of the type which was then, in 1894, in general use for locomotives. In such a boiler the fire gases from the fire box travel through a bundle of steel pipes, and the space between the pipes is filled with the water which is to be converted into steam. The natural steam from a natural steam vent was led through the pipes that normally carried the fire gases.

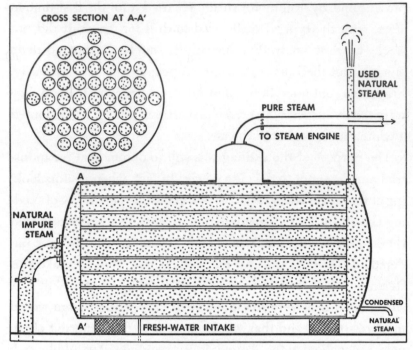

16. Flowsheet of Dr. Raynaut's boiler and steam engine

The heat was sufficient to convert the water in the boiler into steam which drove a steam engine of 9 horsepower in a normal fashion. (See diagram, fig. 16.) It could be done.

Doctor Raynaut's next attempt miscarried, however. The natural steam rushed from the vents with every indication of high pressure; if one placed a paddlewheel in its way one might obtain power directly from such a steam jet, without boilers and expensive machinery. The steam turned the paddlewheel all right, but it also corroded it in a short time.

The experiment was repeated a few years later, in 1897, by Prince Piero Ginori-Conti, who had acquired an interest in the firm, which by then had changed its name to Società Boracifera di Larderello.[2] But Prince Ginori-Conti's paddlewheel became covered with boric acid and corroded just as fast as Dr. Raynaut's wheel. Obviously this method was wrong, at least at Larderello. Much of the failure was blamed on the fact that the steam also carries water droplets with it. The engineers of the Società Boracifera then began to design an apparatus that would trap the water droplets but let the steam pass. They succeeded by 1904 and connected the apparatus with a steam vent, and a ¾-horsepower steam engine with the apparatus. The steam engine was coupled with a small dynamo. It was a small dynamo, all right; it produced just enough current to light five electric lamps. But it worked!

In the following year the company installed a 40-horsepower steam engine, coupled to a dynamo which produced enough power to illuminate the whole factory and the village where the engineers and the workers lived. For some time everybody was pleased no end. The *lagoni* provided a never-ending stream of boric-acid solution as raw material. The *soffioni* furnished the heat for evaporating the solution and now they also provided power for illuminating the place. Add the facts that the whole operation was lucrative and that Chianti was made less than 30 miles away, and you'll agree that there was reason to rejoice.

One day the steam engine stopped. There was no preliminary warning of any kind. It simply stopped. Oiling and superficial maintenance did no good. After a probably prolonged discussion it was decided to take the engine apart. And when that was done the engineer in charge could only wonder why the engine had run as long as it did. All its interior parts were corroded out of shape, eaten up by substances which were carried by the steam

[2] Since 1939 the name has been simply the Larderello Company.

and which had not been eliminated by the separating apparatus that trapped the water droplets—and probably did not do that very well either!

Since that time the steam has been carefully analyzed and its pressure and temperature have also been measured. The "coldest" steam jet emerges at a temperature of 284 degrees Fahrenheit; the warmer steam jets register at around 420 degrees. The pressure at the mouth of a steam jet is around 70 pounds per square inch; if you lead the steam into a closed container pressure will build up to about 400 pounds per square inch. Holes for steam are now drilled to depths of 1200 feet and more. Interestingly enough, neither the pressure nor the temperature of the steam shows any very clear relationship to the depth of the hole. In general, steam from deeper holes tends to be warmer, but not necessarily in proportion to the depth.

As for the impurities carried by the steam, the amount, but not the nature, differs slightly from place to place. At Larderello all the impurities taken together amount to about 6 per cent of the weight of the steam. At Lago they amount to only 4 per cent; elsewhere the amount may be a little less than at Lago or slightly more than at Larderello. At Larderello, the composition of the steam, in 100,000 parts of natural steam (by weight), is as follows:

steam (H_2O)	95,529 parts
carbon dioxide (CO_2)	4,185 parts
methane gas (CH_4) and free hydrogen (H_2)	110 parts
hydrogen sulfide (H_2S)	92 parts
nitrogen (N_2)	30 parts
boric acid (H_3BO_3)	35 parts
ammonia (NH_3)	19 parts

The so-called rare gases, argon, helium, krypton, and xenon, are also represented in the steam but in such minute quantities that their common name, "rare" gases, acquires meaning; all of them taken together amount to roughly 1 part in 100,000 parts of impure natural steam.

To return to the steam engine: 35 parts of boric acid, 92 of hydrogen sulfide, and 19 of ammonia, in every 100,000 parts may not sound like much, but they were enough to ruin any steam engine within a fairly short time. To obtain power without ruining the machinery in the process it was necessary to go back to Dr. Ferdinando Raynaut's original experiment, which utilized not the pressure of the natural steam but its heat. The first modern steam turbogenerator was installed at Larderello in 1913; it was a 300-horsepower turbine driving a 4000-volt, 250-kilowatt generator.

In 1914 three more power-generating units were added, each one with a power output twelve times as great as the first one of 1913. With the installation of these three units electric power from Larderello began to become an economic factor in Tuscany. At first Larderello supplied only itself. Then it furnished current for nearby Volterra, after that for Cecina and Siena, later for Florence and Pisa and Livorno as well, and finally for the Italian State Railways as they gradually began replacing their old coal-burning locomotives with electric trains. The first Italian electric train to use current furnished by the unborn volcano of Larderello was the one on the Florence-to-Rome run.

During the First World War the emphasis at Larderello was on power, but immediately afterward Prince Ginori-Conti began to call on scientists for systematic exploration and on engineers for systematic exploitation. It was obvious that many things could still be done. There was, for example, a new type of turbine available which might be able to utilize the natural steam directly. This did work, but was still not as satisfactory as the other system of using the natural steam to make pure steam of fresh water.

But there was also the composition of the steam to be considered. The natural steam carried a little more than 4 per cent of carbon dioxide. Since this decreased the efficiency of the pure steam boilers to some extent it was desirable to get rid of it before the steam was put to work. But whether one separated the carbon dioxide out of the natural steam while it was still hot or afterward when it was less hot, there were 4 pounds of carbon dioxide available in every 100 pounds of steam which the *soffioni* produced, and they produced many hundreds of pounds of steam every second. Carbon dioxide is itself an article of commerce; it was senseless to waste it by discharging it into the air. In 1930 a factory for making commercially pure carbon dioxide joined the boric-acid refineries and other activities at Larderello. It produced 330 pounds of carbon dioxide every hour, at first in the form of compressed gas in steel bottles, later partly in the form of dry ice.

Chemists and engineers also worked together in the Larderello laboratories to separate the methane gas and the free hydrogen. Both together amount to only $\frac{1}{10}$ of 1 per cent of the steam volume. But the steam volume is large and these gases, when bottled, are important industrial fuels. And the $\frac{92}{100}$ of 1 per cent of hydrogen sulfide can be made into sulfuric acid, which is also a commercial commodity. In short, all the "impurities" of the steam, which had been merely a nuisance at first, are important and worth money, provided you have enough of them. The Larderello experts even go after that 1 part in 100,000 which consists of the rare gases. Most of this part is helium, the ideal gas for inflating balloons and blimps because it can carry almost as much weight as hydrogen but does not burn.

Another direction in which the engineers went to work was toward increasing the supply of water holding boric acid in solution. The *lagoni* were small, but no matter how much water was taken from them they always refilled. Obviously there were subterranean bodies of water with dissolved boric acid. If these could be tapped, the supply of such water would presumably be increased, and in any case the water was not likely to be muddy like that in the *lagoni* at the surface. If one succeeded in finding such a subterranean *lagone* and drilled a hole through the intervening layers of rock the water might rise to the surface by itself. If not, one could pump it out. Or else one could lead steam from a nearby *soffione* into the bore hole and force the water up that way. This project also succeeded.

Then, in 1931, something unforeseen happened.

A new drilling machine—oil-well drilling rotary-type rig, to give it the proper identification—had been at work for several weeks. When work stopped in the evening of March 26 the equipment registered the depth of the hole as 877 feet from the surface. The next morning the well blew, with enough noise to be clearly audible in Florence, some 25 miles away. Fortunately nobody was injured, but the new steam jet was so enormous that nobody believed at first that it could be harnessed. It blew 220 tons of steam into the air every hour, with enough noise to make communication impossible for miles around. The first thing the men on the spot did was to give the jet a new name. This was no longer just a *soffione* such as Nature had made for thousands of years and as men had drilled for over fifty years. This was a *soffionissimo!*

Then they went to work on it, and only 22 days after the blow-out the *soffionissimo* was under control. The second of the *soffionissimi* erupted on April 22, 1932, when, after 4 weeks of drilling, a depth of 695 feet had been reached. It was slightly cooler than the first—356 degrees Fahrenheit as compared to the 402 degrees of the 1931 phenomenon—and also slightly smaller in volume, producing 170 tons of steam per hour. It was under control by May 14, 1932. A third *soffionissimo* erupted in 1936. With this enormously increased steam production all operations grew by leaps and bounds, and in 1939, when the Second World War started, the total of the steam spouting from 140 wells of assorted sizes amounted to 2000 tons per hour.

Larderello was active all through the Second World War until the Allies landed in Italy. The retreating German armies could not hand over a fully functioning power plant, supplying the railroads for many miles around and powering the street cars in half a dozen cities, to the Allies as a gift. It would be like giving an enemy a fleet of tanks, "the better to pursue me with, dear." So the Germans tore the caps off the steam wells and let the steam blow uselessly into the air, dynamited the condenser tower and the dynamos, short-circuited the switchboards, and did, in general, as much damage as time permitted. When the Americans entered Larderello it was "Hell with all the fires still going." The Italian engineers were helpless—how can one repair a factory without power? Finally they discovered a small generator of only 15 kilowatts in a storage shack. It produced just enough power to keep the welding equipment of the repair crews running. After a while the Italians had one of the bigger generators going. American aid in the form of supplies and repair equipment arrived. Two years after the man-made catastrophe Larderello was back to the production norm of 1939. It has expanded since.

But isn't Larderello an engineer's dream already realized?

In a sense it is, but mainly it serves as an indication of what the future can bring. In the first place, of course, there are other areas where the experience gathered at Larderello can be put to work, with or without the accompaniment of the production of commercial chemicals. In Italy itself there is a generally similar area, the *fumaroli* ("smokers") near Naples, close to Mount Vesuvius. In Sicily there is Mount Etna. Then there is Iceland, of course, and there are the hot springs and volcanoes of New Zealand where survey work is now under way.

In New Zealand the Dominion Government appropriated the equivalent of 14 million dollars in 1952 to drill for live steam at the most promising site, the Wairakei Valley. Test bores—twenty-seven of them by the summer of 1953—were drilled to depths as great as 3200 feet. The steam pressure in the Wairakei Valley was found to be generally higher than in Tuscany; the 3200-foot well produced steam with a pressure of 1450 pounds per square inch. So far the New Zealand steam wells do not do any actual work, but the existing steam bores could supply a city of about 200,000 inhabitants, and the total possible output of the valley is likely to be a dozen times as high.

Java is a promising island for such developments; in 1926 several Dutch geologists made a survey of a volcanic area called Kawah Kamondjang for just this purpose and considered it "highly suitable." The Japanese showed much interest in Larderello, but they, as well as the people of Java, were delayed by the Second World War, as were the Icelanders. In North America we have the famous Valley of the Ten Thousand Smokes in Alaska and several spots in the United States proper. One of them, the Mayacama Range not far to the north of San Francisco, was investigated by the General Electric Company as long ago as 1921. The first test wells produced enough steam for a turbogenerator set which then delivered the power to drill additional test holes. But California is not Italy. Italy has no coal at all, no oil, and very little water power. In California coal may cost more than in Pennsylvania, but both oil and water power are available. In short, while a plant like Larderello could be established in California, it probably would not pay at present and might not for decades to come.

But the lesson of Larderello goes far beyond indicating the possibilities of half a dozen areas of similar nature. By demonstrating that the utilization of volcanic heat is possible it has also shown that it is possible, in principle, to tap the heat of the earth's interior.

If you dig a deep shaft or well anywhere, far away from any volcanic activity, you'll find that the temperature increases the deeper you go. The average figure for this increase in non-volcanic areas is 1 degree Fahrenheit for every 60 feet of depth. If you use this figure as a basis you find that there should be an increase of 90 degrees Fahrenheit per mile of depth. At the bottom of a 3-mile shaft you should find a temperature of 270 degrees Fahrenheit [3] and at the bottom of a 5-mile shaft 450

[3] Three miles happens to be the greatest depth at which temperature has actually been measured. A drill hole of this depth exists in Texas but instruments

degrees Fahrenheit. But geologists know of many places where the temperature increases much faster than 1 degree per 60 feet of depth, due to remains of age-old volcanic activity. One of these places has been found near Neuffen in Würtemberg, Germany, where the temperature increases by 1 degree Fahrenheit every 6½ feet. There the rocks at the bottom of a 3-mile hole would have temperatures between 850 and 900 degrees. All this simply means that you can "dig for heat" anywhere, provided you dig deep enough.

The man who first reasoned along these lines was Sir Charles Algernon Parsons, inventor of the type of turbine named after him. If we drive a vertical shaft to a depth at which the heat is great enough for water to boil, he said, we can create artificially the same situation which Nature has produced in Tuscany. To do the job efficiently and well, two shafts would be needed, each a number of yards in diameter and lined with steel plates. One would be the "down" shaft, fed with surface water which should be as clean as possible. On the way down the water would be intercepted at regular intervals by water turbines coupled to generators. At the bottom of the shaft there should be a large cavern which would be the "boiler," heated by the earth itself. The second shaft, steel-lined like the first, would be the "up" shaft, through which the steam would rise, also intercepted at intervals by turbines, but steam turbines in this case.

A calculation made by another author at about the time of Sir Charles's death (1931) ran as follows: We have many surface water-power plants which swallow as much as 350 cubic feet of

---

showed a temperature of "only" 120 degrees centigrade, which is equal to 248 degrees Fahrenheit. Obviously in that locality a little more than 60 feet of depth were required for a rise of 1 degree Fahrenheit.

water per second. If the earth's heat transformed this amount of water into steam of a temperature of 320 degrees Fahrenheit the power output of this one plant would be equal to one-two-hundredth of the power needs of all nations taken together. In other words, if we could build two hundred such power plants they would supply the whole world.

Even if this figure is somewhat low, as appears likely, it indicates an enormous untapped reservoir of power in the earth. The question is whether this power can be tapped, and the answer to that question is "Not yet." Critics of Sir Charles Parsons' idea have mostly stressed the points that we cannot build shafts of the necessary width several miles deep and that it would be impossible to excavate a cavern at the deepest point. Others have replied to these critics by saying that one would naturally not just pick a place at random and then dig 3 or 4 miles until a useful temperature has been reached; one would look for favorable areas like the one in Württemberg. An Italian geologist, the late Ettore Cardani, who specialized in the exploration of Mount Vesuvius, definitely located a large "pocket" of magma underground near that volcano. The upper edge of that pocket is only 800 feet below the surface, and the temperature of the magma is estimated to be 2200 degrees Fahrenheit, so the rocks nearby should have a temperature of about 1500 degrees Fahrenheit.

The problem, of course, is not so much that we cannot drive shafts to a depth of several miles, since we already know areas where we would not have to dig very deep. It is that the work would have to be done with and in rock of a temperature of 320 degrees Fahrenheit, preferably hotter. The vertical shafts probably could be produced by either automatic or remotely controlled machinery. But what about the cavern? It should be large, the larger the better, and how do you dig it by remote control?

Two answers are possible here. One is that we now have instruments that would enable us to find a natural cavern at considerable depth, if there is one, without more digging than is required to reach bedrock. Then it would be necessary only to drive two shafts down. The other answer is that, if we really had to, we might invent machinery which could excavate such a cavern without the need for living operators. The comforting fact is that the energy is there. If we need it, we'll find ways and means of going after it.

4. THE VALLEY OF THE JORDAN

17. The Jordan Valley project

The Valley of the Jordan

The coastline of the eastern end of the Mediterranean Sea is about 450 miles long and runs approximately north and south. The deviation from the meridian is just 120 miles, which in this case means that the northern end is 120 miles farther east than the southern end. The land which bounds the Mediterranean on the east is an ancient plateau and therefore rises rather sharply from the sandy shoreline.

Strangely enough, that eastern shore of the Mediterranean never had a name. On modern maps the northern coastal section of a little over 300 miles is designated as Syria, while the remaining 120 miles in the south are labeled Palestine or Israel. But even these names are fairly new in their modern meaning because originally they were the names of much smaller areas. The term Palestine was not used for the whole land until after the end of the Roman Empire, while Syria as a designation for the area to which it is now applied is hardly a century old.

In the course of human history Syria never played an important role, while the much smaller Palestine to its south is the most famous country on earth. It is the Holy Land where one of the world's great religions was born.

In addition to its religious significance to both Christians and Jews, Palestine is the wonderland of the archaeologist and historian; dig where you will and nearly every acre will yield historical relics, from skulls of men of the Stone Age to artifacts of the time of the Crusades.

But Palestine is also of interest to scientists other than archaeologists and historians. At an average distance of 40 miles from the Mediterranean coast, beyond the hills and mountains, lies the Valley of the Jordan.

The name of the river itself hints at the astonishing fact which geologists unraveled long afterward. "Jordan" means "that which comes down," and this is a literal description. Springing from four small sources, the Jordan becomes a united, though small, river a few miles to the north of a marshy area called Lake Huleh on maps. This marshland, where papyrus grows thickly, is at about the same level as the Mediterranean Sea, but then the Jordan rushes down 680 feet in a distance of only 9 miles to where the valley widens to form the Sea of Galilee (or Lake Tiberias), a roughly triangular body of water measuring 13 miles from north to south and about 8 miles across at its widest point.

South of Lake Tiberias is the Valley of the Jordan proper, called the Ghor, with an average width of about 4 miles. The length of the Ghor, which runs almost precisely north and south, between the southern end of Lake Tiberias and the northern end of the Dead Sea, is 65 miles. At the bottom of the Ghor flows the Jordan, but not in a straight line. It meanders about, in a depression which it has cut into the bed of the Ghor,[1] to such an extent that the length of the river is close to 200 miles. At the

[1] The depression has a name of its own, Zor.

end of the Ghor it empties into the Dead Sea, but while the level of Lake Tiberias, where the Apostles cast their nets, is almost 700 feet lower than that of the Mediterranean, the level of the Dead Sea is 1292 feet below Mediterranean level. The depth of the Dead Sea is surprisingly great too; in its southern portion 1278 feet of water have been recorded. The bottom of the Dead Sea, therefore, is 2570 feet below sea level!

Geologists, amazed by the unheard-of spectacle of such a deep valley near the sea, wondered how far the valley might extend. To the north it could be traced for a comparatively short distance beyond Lake Huleh to a depression between Lebanon and Hermon. In the south its continuation was the Gulf of Aqaba (one of the arms of the Red Sea) and the Red Sea itself. But to find out whether the valley indicated by the Ghor continued still farther southward the geologists had to wait for further information from explorers of Africa. When that information came in they saw that the valley, which meanwhile had been named the Great Rift Valley, indeed continued for thousands of miles.

It runs down through the Red Sea and reappears on the African continent, where its deeper points are filled with water, forming a unique chain of lakes. The northernmost of the lakes of the Great Rift Valley—more precisely, the northernmost depression which contains a lake—is Lake Rudolf, with the respectable area of 3475 square miles. The next one of the Rift Valley lakes is Lake Albert; it is not very deep, with 50 feet about the average, but it has a length of 100 miles and a width of 22 miles. Lake Edward, about 44 miles long, is one of the Rift Valley lakes and so is 62-mile-long Lake Kivu in Ruanda-

Urundi, but the enormous Lake Victoria in the same general area is not.

Lake Victoria—or, as it is often called by retaining the native word for "lake," the Victoria Nyanza—is generally shallow, with a measured maximum depth of 270 feet, and has an irregular shape. Its area of 26,200 square miles makes it one of the world's largest lakes (unless you count the Caspian Sea, only Lake Superior, with 31,810 square miles, is bigger), but it exists independently of the Rift Valley.

To the south of Lake Kivu, the Rift Valley is continued by the two "long" lakes, Tanganyika and Nyasa. And these two are certainly astonishing lakes. Tanganyika is 450 miles long and only 45 miles wide, and Nyasa 350 miles long, with the same greatest width. The levels of both lakes are far above sea level, 2624 feet in the case of Tanganyika and 1645 feet for Nyasa. But both lakes are also enormously deep; the greatest depth of Tanganyika recorded so far is 4708 feet, and that of Nyasa 2580 feet, so that both lake bottoms are far below sea level.

Both lakes are deep, drowned depressions of the Rift Valley. Beyond Lake Nyasa it continues almost due south and finally loses itself in the so-called Mozambique Channel that separates Madagascar from the African mainland.

All these reports from Africa showed the fairly incredible Jordan Valley to be just the northern end of an even more incredible feature of the earth's crust. Geologists had all this information on their charts about half a century ago and because of it they swelled the already large ranks of people interested in Palestine.

In about 1925 a Frenchman, Pierre Gandrillon, pointed out

that the Valley of the Jordan should be of great interest to engineers too. The Jordan Valley was, if you utilized it correctly, the Nature-made "stage set" for a useful and highly interesting feat of engineering.

Gandrillon's reasoning began with an analysis of an ordinary hydroelectric power plant, located at the bottom of any natural waterfall you care to name. The power plant extracts energy from the falling water by means of water turbines which are coupled to generators so that the energy appears as electric current. The waterfall will be the more "powerful" the larger the volume of water that passes over it per second and the faster the water arrives. The speed of fall, of course, is determined by the height of the drop; the higher the drop in feet, the higher the speed of arrival at the bottom in feet per second.

In order to have a waterfall you have to have an inexhaustible supply of water at a high level, normally a river which is replenished all year round by rains and snows. But there must also be some provision for removing the water at the bottom of the waterfall. Normally the water that has gone over the fall is removed by draining to a still lower level, the ocean. But this is not the only way in which the water that has done its job can be removed. It can, in an appropriate climate, be made to disappear by way of evaporation.

In Palestine there is a large natural "evaporating pan," the Dead Sea. Filling what is probably the deepest point of the Great Rift Valley, the Dead Sea is 47 miles long with an extreme width of 9½ miles, giving its surface an area of 340 square miles. Its water is so heavy with dissolved salts that it is impossible for a swimmer to sink and drown. Fish swept into the Dead Sea by the Jordan die very quickly, and in those super-salty waters which exceed the saltiness of the ocean about seven times nothing lives—hence the name. But the waters of the Dead Sea are not concentrated ocean water; the composition is very different. In the oceans the main constituent of the dissolved salts is common table salt, sodium chloride; in the Dead Sea the main ingredient of the saltiness is magnesium chloride, which happens to be more valuable.

TABLE OF SALT CONTENT
(*Figures are percentages*)

	OCEAN	DEAD SEA SURFACE	DEAD SEA 250 FEET DOWN
sodium chloride	2.60	6.11	7.20
potassium chloride	0.07	0.85	1.25
magnesium chloride	0.31	9.46	13.73
calcium chloride	traces	2.63	3.82
magnesium bromide	traces	0.38	0.61
calcium sulfate	0.12	0.11	0.05
others	0.23	—	—
	3.33	19.54	26.66

Great Salt Lake in Utah, it may be remarked in passing, approaches Dead Sea water in saltiness and may ultimately surpass it, since the area of the Great Salt Lake is steadily diminishing. In 1850 it had an area of 1750 square miles, with an average depth of 25 feet; now its area is about 1500 square miles with an average depth of 15 feet. But the composition of Great Salt Lake resembles that of ocean water, and it is not quite "dead," being inhabited by several species of algae, three insects (*Corixa* and the larvae of two flies, *Ephydra* and *Tipula*), and the brine shrimp *Artemia*.

Since the temperature of the Dead Sea basin is always high— between early May and late September you can count on 110 degrees Fahrenheit—the evaporation reaches nearly incredible figures. Averaged over the whole year, the Dead Sea loses more than 3500 cubic feet of water every second! This loss is just about made up by the rivers feeding the Dead Sea, principally by the Jordan. But since it is obvious from old shorelines that the Dead Sea was larger in the past, the Jordan apparently cannot fully replace the evaporation losses every year. During the decade from 1930 to 1940 the level dropped 12 feet and a few inches. However, this recession might not have been caused by lack of supply. Since the Dead Sea is a portion of the Great Rift Valley it is also possible that the drop was caused by more subsiding of the underlying rock strata.

All these physical features are important to Gandrillon's plan, which would utilize them to provide fresh water for irrigation, and also electric power. Both are needed in Palestine. Palestine, or Israel, can live only by means of extensive irrigation, and one can obtain an idea of the intensity with which this goal is pursued when one learns that the irrigated food-producing area increased thirteenfold between 1922 and 1939. But, contrary to a widespread belief, Palestine is not barren because of lack of rain. There are heavy rains during the winter months. In the coastal areas a total of 28 inches of rain is quite normal and it may run as high as 40 inches. The average yearly rainfall for the whole country (except the Dead Sea basin) is 22 inches, which is 7 inches higher than that of southern California. But though there is no lack of rain most of it runs to waste. It quickly percolates through the limestone rock, and the surface soil is merely wetted temporarily. Hence the need for irrigation.

If one built a dam across the Jordan River at a point near its exit from Lake Tiberias all the water which runs down the Jordan Valley would remain in the lake. Right now the greatest lake depth measured is 150 feet, but the lake could be much deeper and much larger since it only partly fills a large bowl surrounded by steep hills, steepest in the east. The enlarged lake could then be the water source for a much expanded irrigation program.

The Jordan itself would temporarily disappear, until the water in Lake Tiberias rose to the point where it would spill over the dam. But the loss of the Jordan River is something which would be mourned far less by the people living in its vicinity than by those living far away, to whom the Jordan is a symbol rather than an actual river. It is, in its present shape, no great asset to Palestine, nor is it in any respect a beautiful or impressive river. The temperature at the bottom of the Ghor is as high as it is in the Dead Sea basin. The river is deep and turbulent when in flood, but in summer it can be forded in half a hundred places. Consequently it is not navigable at any time of the year and no city was ever built on its banks.

Small wonder that the old Hebrew writings did not contain a single word of praise for the Jordan. On the contrary, it is mentioned only as a horrible example, to be contrasted unfavorably with the clear waters of Damascus. This attitude carried over into the Bible too. In the second book of Kings (5:12), the Syrian captain disdains Elisha's advice to wash in the Jordan by saying "Are not Abana and Pharpar, rivers of Damascus, better than all the waters of Israel?"

The Jordan dam is what might be called the irrigation aspect of the Gandrillon plan. Now let us consider the power aspect. A short distance downstream from the proposed dam the bottom of the Ghor is, in round figures, 700 feet below the level of the Mediterranean Sea. The distance from the sea is 25 miles only, but hills intervene. Pierre Gandrillon looked for a route between the Ghor and the sea along which the heights are not excessive and he found one on which the midway point was only 265 feet above the level of the Mediterranean. There he proposed a large reservoir with connections—partly open canals, partly tunnels—both to the sea and to the rim of the Ghor. The reservoir was to be filled with sea water, pumped from the Mediterranean. The water would be taken from the vicinity of Haifa, and lifting it to the reservoir, 12 miles away and 265 feet higher up, would of course be done in a number of steps. There would be four or five pumping stations, each one lifting the water by some 40 or 50 feet into the next higher canal.

The water of this reservoir would be 980 feet above the bottom of the Ghor. It would be sent down through nearly vertical concrete pipes of large size to a hydroelectric power plant at the bottom. Of course lifting water from the sea to the reservoir would require power, but obviously a drop of 980 feet will generate a far greater amount of power than would be needed to lift the water 265 feet, so there would be a large surplus of electric current. After the water had done its work it could be released into the original Jordan bed to make its way to the Dead Sea at the other end of the valley—the "evaporating pan" already mentioned.

But Gandrillon considered this project only as a temporary expedient while the next stage of his plan was being carried out.

This next stage was to build a canal for the sea water which would lead it across the bed of the Jordan into another canal running to the Dead Sea. This second canal would be navigable, carrying both small power boats and freight barges, but it would also serve another purpose. Since it would run to the east of the present river, the canal would stay on a more even level than the river does. When the water in the canal reached the northern tip of the Dead Sea, it would be 590 feet above the sea's level, and another ideal site for a power plant would be created.

This second power plant would be especially important because it could serve the chemical industries near the Dead Sea. Because this body of water provides chemicals in such a high concentration, it is being "mined" for them. Chemical industries always need lots of power, and since there are no fuel deposits anywhere near the Dead Sea the fuel has to be brought there. With a hydroelectric power plant nearby these industries could be enlarged and their production costs lowered. They might even adopt additional processes which are not carried out now because fuel costs are too great.

Remember that the power yield of a waterfall depends on two factors. One is the height of the drop, which in this case is given. The other is the amount of water falling per second, which could be varied. The question which Gandrillon had to ask himself was just how much water one could deliver to the power plants and still be sure that the evaporation from the Dead Sea's surface could dispose of it. It would serve little purpose to provide the chemical industries with cheap current if the production of this same current threatened to drown their installations.

Assuming that 20,000 horsepower should be generated, Gan-drillon calculated that under the prevailing conditions 1100 cubic feet of water had to be taken from the Mediterranean per second. Almost all of this—except for some evaporation losses en route—would end up in the Dead Sea. A first cursory calcula-tion showed that this would cause the Dead Sea to rise about 40 inches per year. But in that first calculation Gandrillon made two assumptions which fortunately happen not to be sound. The first assumption, probably wrong, was that the Jordan River would still be emptying its waters into the Dead Sea; in reality the Jordan would probably be dammed by that time. The second assumption, certainly wrong and made only as a starting point, was that the area of the Dead Sea would not increase with a rise in level. In other words, the calculation was made as if the Dead Sea were a swimming pool with vertical walls. Actually, of course, the Dead Sea is bounded by very gentle slopes of very parched sand all around, so that a rise of only a few feet in level would add enormously to the surface area, and evaporation would increase accordingly.

Under these circumstances—and with the water of the Jordan River stopped short by a dam some 65 miles to the north—it is possible to take enough water from the Mediterranean for a production of 250,000 to 300,000 horsepower without endanger-ing the industrial establishments near the present shores of the Dead Sea.

Very few people called Gandrillon's plan "fantastic" when it was first proposed. That a rising canal with a number of lock gates could be built from the Mediterranean to the rim of the Ghor was not doubted. That the water falling into the Ghor would produce far more electric current than was required to pump it up was obvious. The doubts expressed were financial and political. Even the first power plant would cost quite a lot of money; an investment of several hundred million dollars would be involved. Was this a profitable investment? Who could tell? The main difficulty was political. Palestine was then a British mandate but it began to look as if it might not remain a British mandate. The political future of Palestine was highly uncertain during the period from 1925 to 1935 and nothing was done about Gandrillon's idea.

In 1943–44 an American soil expert, Dr. Walter Clay Lowdermilk, toured Palestine to check on possibilities of improvement. The main problem was, of course, irrigation, but power was required too. Having acquired first-hand knowledge of the physical features of Palestine, Dr. Lowdermilk sat down and evolved an over-all plan for improvement. Although he apparently knew nothing about Gandrillon, the outcome was the same, showing that a scheme of this kind is the logical result of the "lay of the land" in its most literal sense. Of course the "Lowdermilk Plan" —Dr. Lowdermilk himself referred to it as the Jordan Valley Authority, or JVA—differs in some respects from the Gandrillon plan. (See maps, figs. 18 and 19.)

Like Gandrillon, Lowdermilk wanted to take the Mediterranean water near Haifa and lead it through a canal over the Plain of Esdraelon. Like Gandrillon, he wanted to dam the Jordan, but he proposed to put his dam some 10 miles farther south in the Ghor than Gandrillon had suggested. Unlike Gandrillon, Lowdermilk did not want his salt-water canal to cross the Ghor but kept it on the western bank. His reservoir was to be only

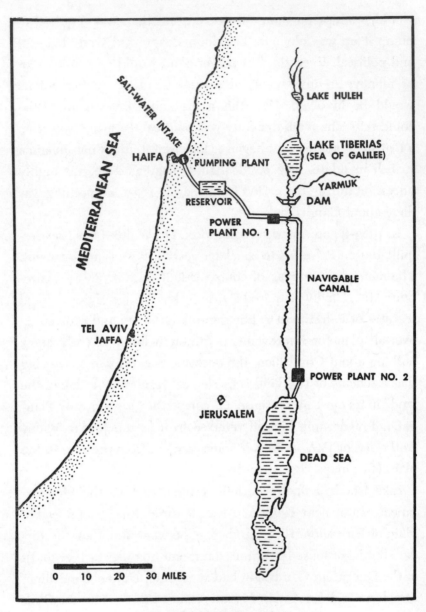

18. The Gandrillon Plan

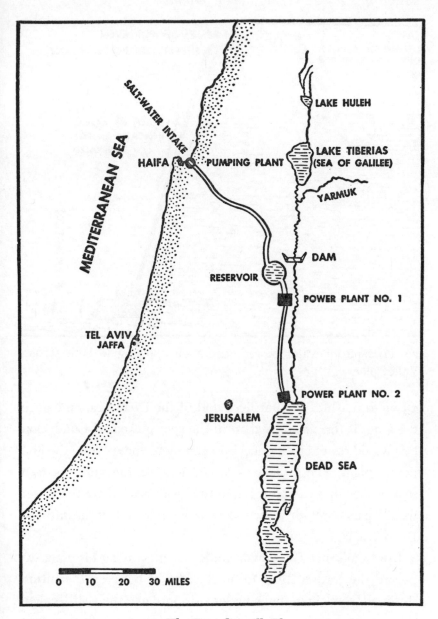

19. The Lowdermilk Plan

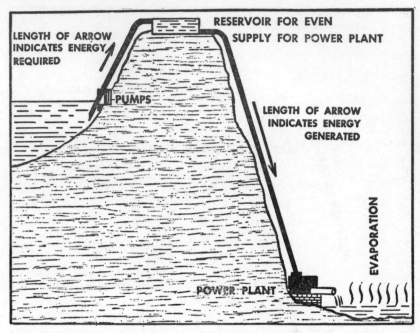

20. Principle of water power generation applying to both Jordan Valley plans

25 miles north of the northern end of the Dead Sea, and since the Ghor is deeper there than in the spot picked by Gandrillon this would result in a higher drop and more energy from the first power plant. The canal was to continue on the same western side of the Ghor until it reached the Dead Sea, where the water would pass through a second power plant and drain into the Dead Sea.

I presume that Dr. Lowdermilk, when evolving his plan, expected the Jordan River to be the border between the future state of Israel and the kingdom of Jordan (then still called Transjordan) and so did not take political border difficulties into account. Unfortunately, when the border between Israel and Jordan was drawn it did cross the Jordan River in a manner which is highly unfavorable for either his concept or Gandrillon's. (See map, fig. 21.)

As things stand now, the former economic difficulties which were in part based on political considerations have changed to

21. The border between Palestine and Jordan, the largest single obstacle in the way of the Jordan Valley plans

purely political difficulties. Nobody doubts that this project could be carried out and that the necessary capital could be found, even though the original estimate of $200,000,000 has been at least doubled. But unless the border is redrawn by mutual agreement, or unless Israel and Jordan proceed in a spirit of wholehearted cooperation, the project will have to be shelved.

In his original study Gandrillon stated that his scheme of producing electricity by water which is then removed by evaporation could also be used in other places besides Palestine. This is of course true; the amusing coincidence is that the most likely other place is in the same general area, in North Africa, about 500 miles to the west of the Dead Sea. The name of this place is the Qattara Depression and it became famous during the Second World War, not because it was the scene of a battle but because it is a place where battle was impossible. The German Afrika Korps under General Rommel was thrusting against Alexandria and was opposed by British forces under Montgomery. Anywhere else in the desert the German panzers as well as the British tanks could have avoided battle simply by veering off. But near El Alamein at the shore of the Mediterranean that was impossible, because the sea was on one side and on the other side was the Qattara Depression which tanks could not enter. The result was the battle of El Alamein, which ended with a British victory.

Strangely enough the Qattara Depression first began to attract attention because of military operations in the First World War. The Libyan Desert to the west belonged to the Italians, who were then on the side of the Allies. The Turks, on the other hand, were allies of Germany. And the Mohammedan fraternity or sect of the Senussi was allied with the Turks and raided Libyan settlements and Egyptian oases. British desert troops, in small units, tried to drive off the Senussi and in the course of these operations the leader of a British desert patrol realized that the Qattara Depression and the oasis Qara were considerably below sea level. After the First World War more attention was paid to the depression because of this discovery, and geographers obtained a complete picture of it.

The Qattara Depression is North African desert at its very worst. It is an enormous expanse of barren sand dunes, alkali flats, and salt plains—some of which are seasonal salt marshes. There are a very few springs and oases near its northern and northwestern fringes. No road crosses the depression, no road even leads to it, but it is crossed in various directions by tracks used by caravans proceeding from rare spring to rare spring.

The depression nestles along the eastern edge of the Libyan plateau with its northernmost point a bare 40 miles from the Mediterranean coast and its extreme eastern lobe stretching to within 130 miles of Cairo. The average width of this enormous basin is 60 miles and its total area is 6950 square miles. This means that the Qattara Depression is almost equal in size to Lake Ontario, which covers 7540 square miles. In general shape, however, it looks more like the much larger Lake Michigan, with a broad base in the south and a narrow end in the northeast. A drive around the depression—difficult to accomplish—would mean a trip of some 700 miles. All in all, it is a basin of respectable size which is shallow merely in proportion to its extent. More than half of its total area lies more than 160 feet below the level of the Mediterranean and near its southern end the bottom is fully 440 feet below Mediterranean level.

An empty basin of the size of Lake Ontario naturally makes one wonder how things would change if that basin contained a lake. A Swiss scientist, Dr. Ball, was the first to propose changing the Qattara Depression into a lake. As has been mentioned, the distance between the northern rim of the depression and the seashore is just 40 miles. There are intervening hills, but they are low, at most a few hundred feet in height. And since the canal bringing sea water to the basin does not necessarily have to be navigable for larger vessels there is no need to cleave down to sea level every hill that is in the way. In some cases it would be easier and cheaper to tunnel through the hill.

As a site for a hydroelectric power plant the drop into the Qattara Depression would be far superior even to the two sites along the Jordan Valley. An achievable drop would be only about 100 feet, but the volume of water that could be utilized would be larger by far. The area of the Qattara Depression has about the same temperatures as the area around the Dead Sea, but not even the smallest river drains into the Depression. Rainfall, of course, is negligible. And the area of the Qattara Depression is roughly twenty times that of the Dead Sea. If we imagine that an earthquake opened a wide chasm from El Alamein to the Qattara Depression, and the waters of the Mediterranean, rushing in, in a fantastic torrent, filled the Depression to the brim, the evaporation rate would still be such that 70,000 cubic feet of water would have to rush through the chasm into the Depression every second just to keep it full. This is about one third of the amount of water that goes over Niagara Falls.

If instead of a natural chasm we build an artificial canal, we would not permit the Qattara Depression to be filled up to the rim; that would curtail electric power generation. A practical method would be to fill the Depression to such a point that its lake level would be 100 feet below the level of the Mediterranean Sea. The area in the Depression then covered by water would be about 3500 square miles, with an average depth of about 100 feet. The evaporation rate from that area would account for a loss of 35,000 cubic feet of water per second—the amount needed to maintain the level. This would also be the amount of water which could be used for generating electric current.

But of course this lake would first have to be formed and, since it would hold an even 10 million million cubic feet, that would take a long time. Let's assume that the filling of the Qattara Depression to the point where its level rises to 100 feet below Mediterranean sea level were done at the rate of 70,000 cubic feet of water per second, the same rate that would flow through a natural chasm to keep the "Qattara Lake" filled.

This would be a flow of 252 million cubic feet per hour or 6048 million cubic feet per day. To fill the Depression to 100 feet below the level of the Mediterranean would take 1653 days or just about 4 years and 6 months, or so it would appear from the simple arithmetic of how soon 10 million million cubic feet of water would accumulate if the water is made available at the rate of 70,000 cubic feet per second. In reality it would take much longer. In the first place a large amount of water would simply disappear into the dry ground. And then, of course, evaporation would occur all the time the Depression was filling up. The fact is that an inflow of somewhat more than 45,000 cubic feet per second could be maintained indefinitely. The very existence of the Qattara Depression insures a large supply of electric current for all time to come.

Unlike most other projects of this kind the "Qattara Hydroelectric Station" would not have any political problems, as the whole area is well inside the borders of Egypt. The two largest Egyptian cities, Cairo and Alexandria, are within 140 miles of the probable site of the power plant, at an easy distance for high-voltage transmission lines. That the Egyptian government is well aware of the existence and value of this unusual natural resource is shown by the fact that, early in 1960, President Gamal Abdel Nasser discussed the idea with Ludwig Erhard, who was then Vice Chancellor of West Germany. As a result of these discussions a team of German engineers was sent to Egypt for a detailed study so that a precise estimate of the necessary investment could be made. The preliminary estimate— before the detailed survey was started—stated that it would cost from 250 million to 400 million dollars.

The problem now is whether Egypt could use the electric current which could be produced; if so, the Qattara Depression will become a lake within the foreseeable future.

5. AFRICA'S CENTRAL LAKE

22. The power plant of the proposed Congo Lake development

Africa's Central Lake

During the Second World War, at the time when the Nazi government of Germany and the Soviet government of Russia maintained an uneasy alliance, the German Foreign Minister Joachim von Ribbentrop approached his Russian counterpart with a strange document. It was a sketchy and obviously hastily drafted proposal concerning "spheres of influence" after the war. The Germans stated that they would let the Russians do whatever they wanted in Asia if Russia would keep hands off Africa completely. Africa, especially Central Africa, the German proposal stated, was of the greatest interest to Germany. Only the northern rim of Africa, bordering the Mediterranean Sea, and some of the northeastern portions, were to be under Italian influence.

The Russians never signed this document and the Germans did not press them very hard, especially since they were at that time preparing for war on Russia. Ever since this proposal became known political observers have wondered why it was made. They seem to have come to the conclusion that it was merely an attempt to sidetrack the Russians.

Maybe so. But it is equally possible that the Germans really did want a free hand in Africa, shared only with their Italian partner, whom they dominated anyway. And they may very well have toyed with the idea of carrying out a project which had been published in German engineering and political journals in 1935, several years before the outbreak of the Second World War. The project in question is quite surprising and very intriguing: it advocates the creation of two enormous fresh-water lakes in the middle of Africa. But it comes under the heading of "politically impossible" unless the African continent is a political unit. At the very least, Central and Western Africa would have to be a political unit; it matters less who rules the extreme southern end of the continent and the northern portions bordering the Mediterranean.

The originator of the project was an architect and engineer named Herman Sörgel who, in 1935, was already well known as the author of another very ambitious idea then called the Panropa Plan (see Chapter 6). What Sörgel said about the possibilities of changing and presumably improving a large portion of Africa reminded some listeners of a much older and rather nebulous idea that had been around, particularly in French magazines and books, three-quarters of a century earlier. Much of Africa was then still being explored, large stretches were still completely unknown, and the explorers reported constant trouble, especially with transportation. The trouble was worst if you were away from a river, and over an area of thousands of square miles in the northwestern portion of Africa there were no rivers whatever. Instead there was the mighty and apparently unconquerable Sahara Desert, an arid region which simply did not end but stretched from horizon to horizon for weeks and weeks of travel.

But whenever you reached the Sahara Desert, whether from the Mediterranean Sea in the north, from the Atlantic Ocean in the west, from the Gulf of Guinea in the south, or even overland from the east, it always seemed as if you, after crossing mountains or at least hills, were descending into the desert. The desert seemed far lower than the surrounding country. It might be below sea level. But if that were the case, all one had to do was to find the portion of the Sahara Desert which most closely approached the sea—probably the Atlantic Ocean in the west—and dig a canal through the hills. It did not need to be a large canal; once the water of the sea had access to the low-lying desert the water itself would do the additional digging. Sweeping into the desert in a ceaseless torrent it would gouge out a channel of considerable width and great depth. In the end, instead of a hostile desert you would have a large and navigable body of water. You could sail in right from the Atlantic Ocean, say somewhere near Cape Blanco (Port Etienne), and reach Morocco and Algeria from the south, the Ivory Coast, Gold Coast, and Nigeria from the north, and possibly Egypt and the Sudan from the west.

A little more exploration showed that this dream of the "Sahara Sea" lacked nothing but some factual background. The enormous Sahara Desert may appear low after you have crossed the Moroccan mountains, but actually only negligibly small areas of the desert are below sea level. Flooding the Sahara Desert with ocean water is simply not possible, since the desert is higher than the ocean. As soon as measurements of the actual elevation of a number of points in the Sahara Desert became available the idea of the Sahara Sea evaporated.

But Herman Sörgel's proposal, even though it reminded some older listeners of the Sahara Sea plan, actually was completely different in concept and much better founded on realities.

To understand his reasoning one first has to gain a general impression of the African continent as a whole. Presenting the over-all shape of a somewhat damaged triangle, Africa stretches 5000 miles from north to south and is almost as wide—4600 miles—from west to east at its widest point. The total area is 11,250,000 square miles. Large figures like that are fairly meaningless by themselves but this particular one means that Africa comprises just about 20 per cent of the total land area of our planet. The average elevation of this huge shield in the earth's crust is 2000 feet above sea level. This same figure also applies to the North American continent, but while North America is generally higher in the west and in the north, the African continent is generally higher in the east and in the south.

It is an interesting feature of Africa that it does not tend much to extremes in its geographical make-up. It has high mountains, but the other large continents boast higher peaks. It has large inland lakes, but not the largest in the world. It has almost the longest river, but only almost, for the Amazon is as long as the Nile and carries more water by far, and the Mississippi-Missouri system is longer. And whether the Sahara Desert is considered larger than the Central Asiatic deserts, or the other way around, is very much a question of definition. However, Africa is the largest stable land mass on our planet. It has remained virtually unchanged over a period of more than 100 million years, its only rival in this respect being Australia, which is much smaller.

The African mountain chains run mostly along the eastern coast, covering enormous areas. There, in this high territory, we have the fantastic deep lakes of the Great Rift Valley; there also are the high peaks of Africa: Kilimanjaro (19,587 feet), Kenya (17,040 feet), and Ruwenzori (16,794 feet). The mountains curve around in the south to the Cape of Good Hope and Cape-town, still 6000 to 8000 feet high. But the mountains in the extreme north of the African continent are not molehills either, a peak near Marrakech, the Toubkal, reaches 13,665 feet into the atmosphere.

Most of the northern part of Africa, from the shore of the Mediterranean Sea to about the fifteenth degree of latitude, is desert, the 3,500,000 square miles of the Sahara. But it is far from being flat, as was once thought, and fairly well near the center of the desert area there are two mountainous highlands. One is the famous Ahaggar plateau with a 9840-foot peak (the Tahat), and the other, a thousand miles to the east, is the Tibesti highland with the Tarso Mountains where volcanic Emi Koussi attains a height of 11,201 feet. But due south of the Tibesti highland there actually is a depression in the desert, the Bodele Depression. And there is a body of water, Lake Chad, finally found in 1823 by Sir Walter Oudney after many centuries of exaggerated, fragmentary, and highly unreliable rumors. The advocates of the "Sahara Sea" derived a lot of comfort from the existence of Lake Chad. Here, it seemed, Nature hinted at what could be done. Actually Lake Chad, although the lowest point of a large depression, is still some 850 feet above sea level.

Lake Chad is the shallow and swampy remnant of what only 10,000 years ago rivaled the 170,000 square miles of the Caspian Sea in area though probably not in depth. What is now left covers some 6000 square miles provided the year is wet, for Lake Chad changes its area, and of course its outline, with the season. At full extent it measures more than 100 miles in either direction, but much of its area is swamp; there are innumerable islands in the lake, and explorers have witnessed with amazement how natives walked from one island to the next, 4 or 5 miles away, without wetting their shoulders. The "deep" portions of the lake seem to average about 20 feet. The only reliable "feeder" of the dying lake is a middle-sized river, the Shari, coming from the south. There are other rivers which empty into the lake, but only for part of the year; at other times they dry up. The Yobe River, which enters the lake from the west, often does not quite make it. It runs along for quite a distance, but evaporation takes its toll and near the lake the sand of the river bed is still moist but there is no running water left.

Strangely enough, this barely existing, if large, lake is only a few hundred miles north of the region of Africa's tropical rain forest, where there is a superabundance of water. This forest is also called the equatorial forest or the Congo forest. All these names are valid because that rain-forest belt coincides fairly well with the line of the equator, and the mightiest accumulation of water in the area is the Congo River. The best condensed description of the area is still that of the late Herbert Lang, who traveled through the rain forest roughly half a century ago for the New York Zoological Society. "The immensity of the wilderness is appalling," he wrote. "For over eighteen hundred miles without a break it stretches more than halfway across the continent, from the coast of Guinea to the Ruwenzori. In spite of tropical luxuriance, it is one of the most dismal spots on the face of the globe, for the torrid sun above miles of leafy expanse, and the unflagging heat of about one hundred degrees day and night, renders the moist atmosphere unbearable. Over the whole area storms of tropical violence thunder and rage almost daily."

Out of this dripping hot rain forest the Congo River comes to the sea, emptying 1,200,000 cubic feet of water into the Atlantic

Ocean every second! More—during the wet season it empties about 1,500,000 cubic feet of water per second. The mouth of the Congo is marked by two "points"; the northern one is named Banana Point, although no bananas grow there, while the southern one, possibly with more justification, is known as Shark's Point. But the brownish waters of the Congo can be clearly distinguished from the blue of the Atlantic 50 miles beyond those two points. Although the Congo is slightly more than 3000 miles long, the distance from its source to its mouth measures only about 1000 miles as the airliner flies. The course of the river as a whole looks like a horseshoe. North of the Congo a part of its horseshoe curve is duplicated by that of the Ubangi River which finally merges with the Congo.

We may as well describe the political situation at this point. The territory inside the double horseshoe of the Congo and the Ubangi—the so-called Congo Basin—used to be the Belgian Congo. The territory east of the horseshoe was British and that to the north and west was French. Now the whole area is independent, but it is not a single nation. The old colonial divisions have to some extent survived in the borders of the new nations. Angola, which is generally south of the Congo Basin but juts into the interior of the horseshoe in one area, is still Portuguese. The most valuable portion of the former Belgian Congo, the High Katanga, is outside the horseshoe-shaped basin.

For several good reasons the Congo River is subdivided into the Upper, Middle, and Lower Congo. The Upper Congo flows almost due north, in the direction of the equator. Just a few miles south of the equator, the series of cataracts known as Stanley Falls begins. The first five falls are very near one another, all occurring within 9 miles. The sixth cataract is 22 miles downstream from the fifth, and the seventh, which is the highest, is 26 miles downstream from the sixth. The total drop of all seven falls is only 200 feet, but they are an impressive spectacle because of the large volume of water that flows over them. As an obstacle to navigation they are as effective as Niagara Falls. And in the course of jumping these cataracts the river has turned west, and at Stanleyville is flowing due west.

It has now become the Middle Congo, which describes a long arc to the north that carries it slightly more than 2 degrees of latitude beyond the equator. It crosses the equator again 630 miles downstream from Stanley Falls; measured along the equator the distance between the two crossings is 472 miles. For most of this stretch the river is 5 to 7 miles wide, with shallow banks, and innumerable islands, many of them several miles long and some much longer. Soon after recrossing the equator the Congo is joined by one of its biggest tributaries, the Ubangi River. The width of the combined rivers is fully 8 miles for a while; then steep hills confine the stream to a bed "only" 2 miles wide, but after a few minor cataracts it widens again to about 6 miles.

Then follows a very interesting stretch, some 120 miles long, which has received a name of its own, the Chenal. Hills with almost vertical faces force all the combined water of the Congo and of numerous tributaries, some of them mighty rivers in their own right, into a channel which is hardly more than 2 miles wide at any point and in places as narrow as 1 mile. But it is just in the Chenal section that the Congo receives one more big tributary, the Kwa River, which forces its way (flowing at right angles to the Congo) through the hills in a 2000-foot-wide chasm. After this confluence—which is called Kwamouth—the Chenal continues for another 60 miles and then widens into a lake which, like the Falls much farther upstream, is named after Sir Henry Morton Stanley. It appears on maps as Stanley Pool. On the maps this area is marked by two city names, Leopoldville on the Belgian side and Brazzaville on the French side.

Below Stanley Pool the river has to force its way through more mountains; in the course of the following 200 miles it forms thirty main rapids and many subsidiary ones, with a total drop of 800 feet. The end of the drop is reached near the town of Matadi. Then the river, now the Lower Congo, slows down and widens out for the remaining 85 miles of its journey, forming a mangrove-bordered estuary. But even there it is not as wide as it was farther upstream; the distance between Banana Point and Shark's Point is only 7 miles.

South of the Congo Basin the African continent is a kind of repetition on a less enormous scale of the features north of the rain forest. The main modification is the presence of the Zambesi River. But the Kalahari Desert is there as a counterpart to the much bigger Sahara in the north, and as the continent began with the Moroccan mountains in the north so it ends with mountains in the south.

Herman Sörgel's project, to which we can now return with much better understanding, is based on one main fact. Quite recently, as geologists count time, the Congo Basin, bounded by rolling country with elevations of from 3000 to 5000 feet and in the east by plateaus 6000 feet and more above sea level, was an inland sea, or, more accurately, an inland lake, since it was fresh water. The level of this lake was somewhat more than 1000 feet above sea level. The lake did not drain into the ocean until the Congo had succeeded in breaking through the hills and mountains which bounded it. Sörgel's suggestion was simply to restore the Congo Basin lake. Block the Congo somewhere in the Chenal and the old lake will fill up again.

In the Chenal the river is only a mile wide in places but it is running fast. This difficulty, however, could be overcome. One way would be to begin by choosing the site for the dam, which would be located below Kwamouth and above Stanley Pool, probably nearer to Stanley Pool. Then one could blast the hills in several places upstream from the dam site. The falling hills would stop the flow of the river for some time, or at least reduce it very considerably. During this time a preliminary cofferdam could be constructed and the real dam built at greater leisure.

The waters of the Congo, the Kwa, the Ubangi, and many other lesser rivers would then slowly drown the Basin, that area of unflagging heat and of insect-borne diseases: yellow fever, malaria, and sleeping sickness. At its maximum extent the lake would cover 350,000 square miles—the combined area of California, Nevada, and Oregon. It would cover only about one-quarter of the area drained by these river systems but would be a very substantial lake nevertheless.

What would happen when the lake had been filled? In the first place one could establish drainage "holes" at strategic points around the lake, each drainage "hole" consisting of a number of nice concrete tunnels 20 or 30 feet in diameter with turbogenerators at the other end. But Sörgel had in mind one specific place for the main drainage. He wanted to place it somewhere north of the point where the Ubangi River makes its sharp turn. The place is situated in the Ubangi Shari. Water drained out of the Congo Lake in that area would run in a northwesterly direction and join the Shari River, the main feeder of dying Lake Chad. There would be enough water not only to stop the shriveling up

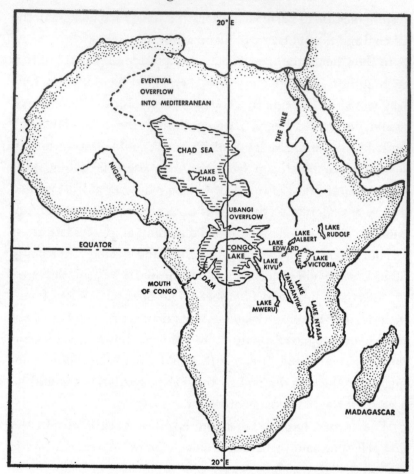

23. Africa as it would look if the Congo Lake and the Chad Sea were realities

of Lake Chad, but, in time, to restore the original Chad Sea, as it was 10,000 years ago.

We know comparatively little at the present moment about the geology of these two original superlakes in Africa, the Congo Lake and the Chad Sea. All we are really sure about is that they existed. It is not at all impossible that their drying up was connected, meaning that the fact that the Congo found a way to the ocean not only emptied the Congo Basin but also deprived the Chad Sea of its main source of water. If that view is correct the whole project would merely restore conditions as they were 10,000 and more years ago.

Now the present Lake Chad does not have any drainage to the sea. It is fed by the Shari and intermittently by other rivers but it loses its water by evaporation. As the water from the Congo Basin gradually restored the old Chad Sea there would come a time when this sea would require a connection with one of the oceans. At some time it simply would have to overflow in some direction. If water has to have an outlet it is always wise to provide one; otherwise it may go in a direction which, though predictable, may be undesirable. Sörgel found that one long extension of the Chad Sea would reach close to the Ahaggar plateau. He planned an outlet from that extension, a river leading northwest past the Ahaggar plateau, curving north into Algeria, and then going almost due east through Tunisia to terminate in the Gulf of Gabès in the Mediterranean Sea. This river could probably be made navigable for small steamers and power boats so that the dream of the Sahara Sea of a century ago would be fulfilled to some extent: one could reach the Ahaggar plateau by boat from the Mediterranean along this "Second Nile" (as Sörgel called it) and then go on across the Chad Sea to Ubangi.

After admitting that this project is far from being as definite in detail or as advanced as, say, the Channel Tunnel or the Jordan Valley projects, let's ask a number of critical questions.

The first one is, of course, whether it can be done at all. This question could really be answered only by a detailed survey, made on the spot for the purpose. But the probability that it can be done is high because it consists essentially of blocking a gap in an existing barrier. And a 2-mile dam should not be too great a problem.

The second question is whether the project is worth the effort. Again the answer is: in all probability, yes. Even now we have not actually conquered the rain forest; we merely avoid it by flying over it. A projected railroad is to go from the valuable High Katanga plateau to the east coast of Africa. Another projected railroad is to go from Brazzaville to the interior of the Basin. But these railroads are mere projects too. If the Congo Basin were water-filled, steamers could go from the vicinity of Brazzaville to the High Katanga, which would certainly be cheaper all around.

The third question is whether land of value might be drowned. This is more difficult to answer than the others. Starting at the end with the "Second Nile" which would empty into the Gulf of Gabès, one can say without hesitation that this river would be useful. As far as the area to be drowned in the Chad Sea is concerned, one can say with equal certainty that every square mile covered with water would be a gain. Unfortunately these two definitely useful stages are the last ones of the whole project. The Shari River will not get any reinforcements of Congo water until the Congo Basin is full. I have not been able to find an estimate of how long this will take, but it obviously is not a question of 3 or 4 years. From the completion of the dam to the appearance of the Second Nile in Tunisia might well be half a century. As for the Congo Basin itself, we don't know whether anything of value would be drowned or not. As far as the map tells the story, everything of known value, and this includes even National Parks and spots of great scenic beauty, would be outside the limits of the drowned area. That the drowned area is an especially unhealthy place is generally conceded, but it is the home of a large number of Africans, about two million, who would have to be moved. Since the property of these Africans is mainly portable property, since the change would come about rather slowly, and, most important, since the move would certainly better their living conditions, it is unlikely that they would object. Moreover, since they are now independent, the order to move would no longer come from a European power (whose intentions may be disbelieved) but from their own government.

Still, the new independence of these people does not simplify the problem. It has been pointed out that the really valuable area of the Belgian Congo was the healthy and sparsely wooded High Katanga plateau, which has rich copper, tin, and cobalt mines, not to mention the richest-known uranium mines. The land of known value was a part of the political unit, but outside the presumably fairly useless Congo Basin. But now the former Belgian Congo is hardly a political unit anymore, and the Africans of the High Katanga are very well aware of the fact that their area produces more cobalt than the rest of the world and that its production figures of copper, gold, zinc, cadmium, manganese, columbium, and tantalum are respectable percentages of the world production. Hence they feel that they have much to gain if they could form a nation by themselves, apart from the poor area encircled by the Congo River.

If they succeed, the remainder of the Congo nation would have very little reason for carrying out the Congo Lake plan; they would sacrifice a large portion of the land area to improve the climate of the adjacent areas and to make the shipping of products easier for the others.

But political situations do change. A decade from now the plan can be discussed once more, after the turmoil of independence has settled down.

6. ATLANTROPA—
THE CHANGED MEDITERRANEAN

24. The Gibraltar dam, as planned by Herman Sörgel

Atlantropa—
the Changed Mediterranean

Ever since the first long canal was dug, the first big bridge put up successfully, and the first tunnel finished, modern man has found it difficult to look at a map without considering whether something else could or should be done. To set the imagination working, a geographical feature on a map needs only to be narrow. There is that narrow piece of land separating the Red Sea from the Mediterranean Sea; result, the Suez Canal. There is the narrow strip of land tying North and South America together; result, the Panama Canal. There is in Greece the narrow Isthmus of Korinthos (Corinth) separating the Gulf of Korinthos from the Gulf of Aigina; the Corinth Canal was the inescapable consequence.

The separating element may also be a narrow strip of water, say the East River between Manhattan and the tip of Long Island; the Brooklyn Bridge was built to span it. And if we return to the Mediterranean Sea, where narrow strips of land led to the Suez Canal and the Corinth Canal, we also find narrow strips of water around it, in a highly interesting and most challenging distribution.

At the eastern end of the Mediterranean Sea the small Sea of Marmara lies between the Aegean Sea, a northern tongue of the Mediterranean east of Greece, and the Black Sea. Both ends of the Sea of Marmara are decided narrows. At the western end there are the Dardanelles, a natural channel some 47 miles long, which has an average width of 3 to 4 miles but is less than a mile wide at one point. At the eastern—or, better, the northern— end of the Sea of Marmara is the strait which we call by the Greek name of Bosporus but which the Turks, who own it, call Istanbul Bogazi. It is 18 miles long, and almost 3 miles wide at the northern entrance. But it has a narrowest point with a width of only 2400 feet, with a strong current running from the Black Sea into the Sea of Marmara and on into the Mediterranean. At the southern end of the Istanbul Bogazi there is Istanbul on one side and Scutari and Kadikoi on the other side. The width at that point is a little less than a mile.

Decidedly this is a place which gives one the feeling that something ought to be done. In about 1875 one J. L. Haddan, who was then director of public works at Aleppo in northern Syria, proposed a tunnel; a bridge of the necessary length was impossible then. He even built a model of the strait and of his tunnel, but the Turkish government of the time would have nothing to do with it. The plan was rejected for political reasons, but this was not stated; instead, Haddan's plan was branded as a "wild and impossible dream." It was not; such a tunnel could have been built. Much later (1949) an American engineer named Charles Andrew again suggested a tunnel under the Bosporus. The Turkish government remained noncommittal. It now looks as if they had already decided in favor of a bridge, because in July 1953, at the request of the Turkish government, the German firm of Stahlbau Rheinhausen submitted a plan and a bid for a bridge. The plan calls for a suspension bridge for automobiles and pedestrians (no railroad), with a length of 4550 feet.[1] But even if the bridge is started at once it will take 5 years to finish.

Moving westward in the Mediterranean area, we find another narrow strait near the middle of the sea. It is the Strait of Messina, with Sicily on one side and the Italian province of Reggio di Calabria on the other. About 50 years ago some not very definite plans for a tunnel were under discussion, but these have been finally abandoned recently in favor of a plan for bridging the Strait of Messina. A design was prepared in 1953 by the late Dr. David B. Steinman of New York City, at the request of the Italian Steel Institute. The bridge would not have to be much longer than existing bridges, but one of the difficulties is that, in the Strait of Messina, it is not only the waters which are turbulent. The ground is earthquake territory—one of the most destructive earthquakes of this century is actually labeled the Messina earthquake. And violent windstorms are almost the rule in winter. Taking all these conditions into account, Dr. Steinman proposed a specially designed suspension bridge, similar in general shape to the George Washington Bridge. The span between the two towers would have to be 5000 feet, some 800 feet longer than the span of the Golden Gate Bridge. The two side spans, between the towers and the land, would each have to be 2400 feet long or about the length of the side spans of the largest bridges now in existence.

The western end of the Mediterranean is even more intriguing.

[1] The George Washington Bridge in New York has a length of 3500 feet; the Golden Gate Bridge in San Francisco a length of 4200 feet.

Again we have the picture of two mighty land masses approaching each other until they almost touch. Almost, but not quite; they are separated along a 30-mile length by the Strait of Gibraltar. This opening, also characterized by a strong current flowing into the Mediterranean Sea, is considerably larger than the narrow straits at the eastern end. Its entrance, coming from the Atlantic Ocean, is more than 25 miles wide but narrows to about 7½ miles. What makes it so impressive is that it is flanked by two remarkable mountains, the Rock of Gibraltar on the north and Djebel Musa on the south. To the ancients these were the Pillars of Hercules. One version of the story has it that Hercules, having been sent to Spain to perform one of his superhuman labors, erected these two "pillars" to mark his travels; another version, a bit more specific, states that Hercules made these two pillars by cleaving a single mountain into two.

That latter version may even be true, provided you substitute the force of Nature for the strength of the son of Alcmene. It is certain that the Strait of Gibraltar did not exist in the far past, but nobody can tell with any certainty when it came into existence, or whether the break between the two continents occurred suddenly or was a slow sinking or disintegration that took many thousands of years.

Naturally (I am tempted to say) the Strait of Gibraltar has its tunnel plan, just like the English Channel and the Bosporus. The Gibraltar tunnel was worked out by a French engineer named Berlier. Because the strait happens to be especially deep at its narrowest point, the location chosen for the tunnel is from Tangier on the African side to a point west of Tarifa on the European side (see map, fig. 25.) The actual shore-to-shore distance along that line is 20 miles, but the tunnel would have to be 25 miles long. It would have to go rather deep, requiring long approaches, with the center section 1500 feet below sea level. Berlier's tunnel does not create a political problem, since both ends would be on Spanish territory. Whether a group of banks could be convinced

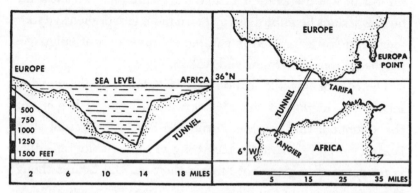

25. The Strait of Gibraltar and the Berlier tunnel: cross section (left) and map (right)

that it is an economic necessity and would therefore prove profitable is a different question.

However, all these tunnel and bridge plans are comparatively minor projects in relation to the Mediterranean Sea, which because of its peculiar structure, shape, and location has really caused people to think.

It was in March 1928 that scientists and engineers first read, with intense amazement, about a plan outlining what could conceivably be done with the Mediterranean. The author was Herman Sörgel, whose Congo plan is described in Chapter 5. Nothing much was known about him at the time, except that he was an architect employed by the government of Bavaria.

At first Sörgel called his scheme the "Panropa Plan"; later, presumably to avoid confusion with a similarly named political association aiming at European confederation, he changed the name to "Atlantropa Plan." The magnitude of Sörgel's proposal was such that some readers wondered whether he was actually serious or was engaged in a huge if obscure joke. To show that he was serious he published in 1929 a more comprehensive statement which was printed in parallel columns in four languages: English, French, German, and Italian.

The title of this publication was *Mittelmeer Senkung*, which means "Reduction of the Mediterranean." Sörgel began with the statement that the Mediterranean Sea in its present shape is a recent body of water. According to some geologists—there is no complete agreement among them on the figures though they are agreed on the facts—about 50,000 years ago the level of the Mediterranean was about 3000 feet lower than it is now. Since 44 per cent of the area of the present sea is less than 3000 feet deep, the ancient sea was obviously much smaller. In fact, there was no Mediterranean Sea then, but only two large lakes, one of them east and one west of present-day Italy-Sicily. Europe was connected with Africa by three wide land bridges, one from present-day Spain to Morocco, one from Tunisia to Sicily and Italy, and one from Greece across the eastern end of the present sea. Later, when the glaciers of the Ice Age melted away, a great deal of fruitful and possibly even inhabited land was drowned. If we want to, said Sörgel, we can get much of this drowned land back. All we have to do is to revoke the alleged feat of Hercules and plug the Strait of Gibraltar with an enormous dam.

It is an undisputed fact that the Mediterranean would shrink visibly if the Strait of Gibraltar were filled in, say, for argument's sake, by an earthquake. The Mediterranean is large, comprising a total of 970,000 square miles, just about ten times the area of the State of Wyoming. It is a warm sea, which means that much of its water is evaporating constantly. The evaporation losses are so high that the level of the sea would recede 5½ feet per year if the water were not replaced. The total mass of water which evaporates from the surface of the Mediterranean every year is a staggering figure—4144 cubic kilometers, which is 146,343,000,000,000 cubic feet! [2]

Actually of course the level of the Mediterranean Sea does not recede because the evaporation losses are made up in various ways. Rain which falls into the sea replaces just about a quarter of the loss. Rivers also help, though not very much, since most of the rivers which empty into the Mediterranean are small and some of them are even seasonal. Only four of them can be called large, the Nile from Egypt, the Po from Italy, the Rhone from France, and the Ebro from Spain. The balance is maintained by water from the Black Sea and the Atlantic Ocean, hence the strong currents in the straits at both ends of the Mediterranean. The contribution of the Atlantic Ocean, which replaces two-thirds of the evaporation losses, results in a flow through the Strait of Gibraltar of 88,000 cubic meters (or 3,100,000 cubic feet) per second, which is twelve times the amount of the waters falling over Niagara Falls at high water!

[2] A cubic kilometer is 1,000,000,000 cubic meters and each cubic meter equals 1.3079 cubic yards, or 35.314 cubic feet. A cubic yard equals 27 cubic feet.

In figures, the contributions of these four sources to the water budget of the Mediterranean are as follows:

| | AMOUNT PER YEAR | | |
SOURCE	*(cubic kilometers)*	*(millions of cubic yards)*	PERCENTAGE
Atlantic Ocean	2762	3,612,000	66.65
rain	1000	1,308,000	24.11
rivers	230	301,000	5.56
Black Sea	152	199,000	3.68
Total	4144	5,420,000	100.00

This table is the basis of the Atlantropa Plan.

Obviously nothing can be done about the rain, and the rivers may as well be left alone. But it would be easy to build a dam across the Dardanelles. By itself this dam would not do any good because the Atlantic Ocean would simply provide an additional 200,000 million cubic yards per year. Still, Sörgel proposed to start at that end, largely because there would be no water-level difference on that dam during construction.

The big job would be the Gibraltar dam. Like Berlier's proposed tunnel, the dam is not planned to cross the strait at its narrowest because the depth there is more than 1600 feet. It would have the shape of a horseshoe, with its open end toward the east. Along the proposed curve of the dam there are many shallow places and the deepest point is about 1000 feet below sea level. The length of the dam would be 18 miles; its crown would be 165 feet wide but its foundation would have to have ten times that width to withstand the water pressure that would soon develop. The estimate of a drop of 5½ feet per year in the level of the Mediterranean is based on the assumption that the sea would receive no water from any source. Since the rain and the rivers would still provide some, the actual recession of the level would be about 40 inches per year. But this would cause a drop of 33 feet within 10 years after the completion of the dam, and this is enough of a difference in level to be utilized to produce electric current—and, considering the amount of water which could be sent through the turbines, to produce it in quantity.

In drawing up the plan, Sörgel did not think in terms of years, and only rarely in terms of decades, but often in terms of centuries. One century after the completion of the Gibraltar dam the level of the Mediterranean Sea would have gone down 330 feet, and by that time a total of 90,000 square miles of new land would have appeared above the surface, with the gains almost proportional for most of the countries bordering the sea. Spain's largest gains would be in the area of the mouth of the Ebro River, France's largest gains in the area of the mouth of the Rhone River. The two islands Mallorca and Minorca would have become one, as would Corsica and Sardinia. Italy would have gained on both coasts, and most of the northern end of the Adriatic Sea would have become the Adriatic Land. Sicily would have grown enormously, and Tunisia too; they would almost but not quite touch. A strait would also still remain between Italy and Sicily but it would be a very narrow one.

From that point on, a further reduction of the sea's level would have little effect on the western part of the Mediterranean but much more on the eastern part. So Sörgel proposed as the second step, a hundred years after completion of the Gibraltar dam, two more dams: one across the remaining narrow strait between Sicily and Italy, say between Messina on the island to a point north of Reggio di Calabria on the toe of the Italian boot;

the second to bridge the gap still remaining between Sicily and Tunisia.

After these dams were completed, the western half of the sea would be stabilized by permitting enough water to enter from the Atlantic to maintain that level. The eastern half would be permitted, in the course of another century, to sink for an additional 330 feet, which it would do all the more readily since virtually its only source of supply would be the Nile. Then the eastern half would also be stabilized, partly with water from the Sea of Marmara and hence from the Black Sea, partly with water from the western half. When completely adjusted in accordance with this plan, the Mediterranean Sea would hold 350,000 cubic kilometers less water than it does now. This amount of water would be distributed over all other oceans, since they are all interconnected, and would raise the sea level everywhere else by 3 feet.

In the Mediterranean area the final result would be 220,000 square miles of new land and hydroelectric power plants of virtually unlimited capacity in a number of places well distributed over the area: at least two in the Gibraltar dam, one each at the mouths of the Ebro, Rhone, Po, and Nile, at least one in the Dardanelles dam, and a minimum of two each in the two dams separating the western half of the sea from the eastern half. There would certainly be no lack of power for anything the inhabitants of the area might wish to do.

Sörgel considered that the final goal of the Atlantropa Plan was the fusion of the European and African continents; he entitled a later book (published in 1938) *The Three Big A's—* America, Asia, and Atlantropa. But he also repeatedly pointed out that his plan could be stopped at any moment after the level of the sea had dropped, say, 50 feet, and still realize its chief purpose. Such a comparatively small reduction of the sea's level might not provide much new land, or any land of value, but it would create the means of producing enormous amounts of electric power.

If Sörgel's main idea—the dams across the Dardanelles and the Strait of Gibraltar—is ever carried out it is highly probable that the men entrusted with the Atlantropa project will stop when the sea level has fallen 50 or 75 feet. (This drop would be accelerated if the Gandrillon Plan for Palestine and the Qattara Depression plan, described in Chapter 4, were carried out simultaneously, since both take water from the Mediterranean.)

It is important to remember that none of this must interfere with shipping. Damming the Dardanelles might not be hard, but ships still would have to get from the Mediterranean to the Sea of Marmara and the other way round. For this, canals would have to be built, with a series of lock gates to take care of the difference in level. The Suez Canal would have to be lengthened and locks built at the Mediterranean end, and, most important, canals and locks would be required for the connection between the "inner sea" and the Atlantic Ocean.

The Gibraltar locks especially would have to be large enough to accommodate the largest ocean liners, battleships, and aircraft carriers. Every additional 50 feet of level difference to be overcome means one more lock in each canal and adds considerably to the length of the canal. The biggest gain would actually be made by the first 50 feet of level drop. This drop would

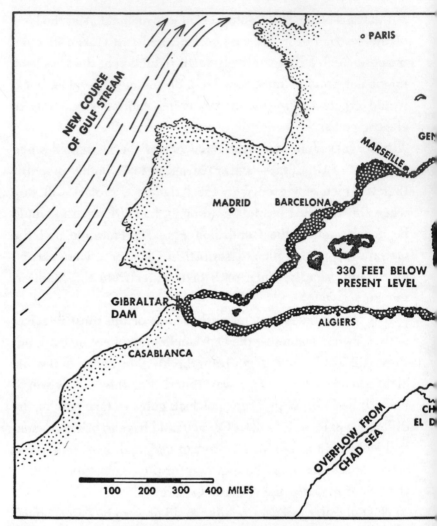

26. The Mediterranean Sea, showing the full extent of the Atlantropa Plan, after the eastern half has evaporated to a level 660 feet below the present level. The western half will be maintained at a level 330 feet below the present level. The black areas show the land that would be above the new sea levels.

provide power without doing too much harm to existing installations.

It would also accomplish something else which has not yet been mentioned. The figure of 3,100,000 cubic feet per second for the inflow through the Strait of Gibraltar represents the dif-

ference between two flows which take place there. At the surface
the influx of water from the Atlantic is greater than that figure,
but at the bottom there is, according to Sörgel, a flow in the
opposite direction which brings cold bottom water from the
Mediterranean into the open sea. This outflow is accused of
forming a cold-water cushion outside western Europe which
deflects the Gulf Stream into the northern Atlantic. Presumably,
if this cold-water cushion were absent, the Gulf Stream would
flow into the English Channel and thereby warm northern
Europe more efficiently. A dam across the Strait, stopping any
flow in either direction, would take care of that.

The reason many European experts who have studied the
Atlantropa Plan, and many who are very much in favor of it,
would like to stop after 12 or 15 years is that the continuation
would prove costly. If the Mediterranean level were lowered
60 to 75 feet, about the only extra expenses required would be
for equipping the Suez Canal with a lock somewhere near Port
Said and deepening the Corinth Canal. But once the recession
of the level goes beyond 100 feet, every single harbor along the
shores of the Mediterranean stops being a harbor. Barcelona,
Marseille, Genoa, Naples, Taranto, Trieste, Fiume, Haifa, Tel
Aviv, Jaffa, Alexandria, Bengasi, Tunis, Bizerte, Algiers, Beirut,
and Oran—to name only the larger ones that come to mind at
once—would all be miles from the sea. Some of them might be
"salvaged" by means of canals to the new shoreline, but many
would become completely worthless, at least as harbors. Obviously, beyond a certain point the plan runs into the law of
diminishing returns.

Another serious argument for stopping the Atlantropa Plan at
an early stage is the volcanism of the Mediterranean area. Even

now conditions are not as stable there as one would wish and it is feared that removal of the weight of water from these unstable areas may lead to earthquakes and volcanic eruptions. This, of course, is a field in which nobody can claim to have experience. It is possible that such fears are unfounded, but it is by no means possible for anybody to claim that they *are* unfounded. However, it seems logical to assume that the danger would increase roughly in proportion to the weight of water removed and that the results of a minor reduction in sea level would be minor too.

Of course under present conditions the Atlantropa Plan is politically impossible. It would need the cooperation of more than a dozen different nations. Some, such as Spain and Italy, would gain relatively much, while others would actually lose something; England, for example, would lose control of the Strait of Gibraltar. It is therefore unnecessary to discuss the engineering difficulties involved in the construction of a dam of such magnitude as the Gibraltar dam. The political situation of today makes the engineering problems future problems, and we can't tell how an engineer 50 years from now would go about solving them.

There can be no Atlantropa until a united Europe is a reality and until the control of the Strait of Gibraltar has developed into a purely commercial problem, with all military aspects absolutely missing.

Interestingly enough, the situation which prevails for the whole Mediterranean also holds true for a much smaller body of water in its immediate neighborhood—the Red Sea, part of the Great Rift Valley.

The Red Sea is, in round figures, 1200 miles long, and on the

average less than 200 miles wide, except in its southern part
where a maximum width of 250 miles occurs. Its surface has an
area of about 180,000 square miles. The land bounding it along
both shores is desert. Its northern end is closed except for the
one artificial opening of the Suez Canal. Not a single river
empties into the Red Sea. Its southern end is the sharply con-
stricted Strait of Bab el Mandeb, which is further narrowed by
the existence of the British-owned island of Perim, which divides
the strait into two channels. The one to the east of the island is
2 miles wide, the one to the west 16 miles.

Since the Red Sea is a part of the Great Rift Valley it is much
deeper than one would expect. The average depth is 1600 feet,
but a number of extra-deep depressions have been measured, one
of 4200 feet and one even of 7200 feet.

The "Red Sea Plan," worked out by the French engineer
René Bigarre and published in 1940, shows many similarities to
the Atlantropa Plan, with some features of Dead Sea development projects thrown in. It simply consists of a dam across the
Strait of Bab el Mandeb with Perim as an off-center anchor.
Naturally there would have to be a canal with lock gates connecting the Gulf of Aden with the Red Sea, and the Suez Canal
would also need a lock gate at the Red Sea end, in the vicinity
of Suez. After these had been built, evaporation could take its
course. It is so enormous there that Matthew F. Maury, a United
States naval officer whom many call the Father of Oceanog-
raphy, estimated a century ago that the level of the Red Sea
would sink 23 feet a year if no water could come in from the Gulf
of Aden and the Indian Ocean.

René Bigarre thinks Maury's estimate too high and counts
on only 0.4 inches per day or slightly more than 12 feet per year.

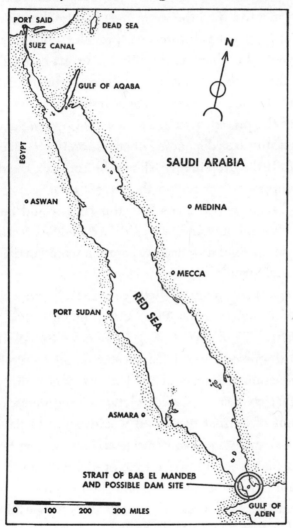

27. The Red Sea

Even this is enormous, amounting to a removal of 153,200 million cubic feet per 24-hour period. If Bigarre's figures are right, power generation could start about 5 years after completion of the dam; if Maury's should be correct, it could start in 2 years and a few months. If all the water then required to maintain the Red Sea at its new level were sent through turbines, the power output would be about 240 million kilowatt-hours daily. To produce that much by means of steam turbogenerators you would have to burn 200,000 tons of coal daily!

Some of the present Red Sea area would become dry land in the process, the area depending of course on the total level drop permitted. If the drop in level should be 100 feet, the dry areas would comprise 10 per cent of the present total area of the Red Sea, possibly 12 per cent. As land this land would be useless; as a source for salt it would be useful. The Red Sea is saltier than the open ocean right now and evaporation would make it saltier still. The yield would run into millions of tons.

From almost any angle the Red Sea Plan looks like a miniature version of the Atlantropa Plan. Carrying out Bigarre's plan would virtually provide a testing ground for Sörgel's ideas. It has been discussed recently in greater detail by Professor El Sayed Mohammad Hassan of the University of Cairo who calculated that six years after completion of the dams and locks the amount of current generated would begin to pay enough to meet the expenses of maintenance and replacement of equipment, but that it would take a total of eighty-two years to pay off the entire investment plus accumulated interest.

The Red Sea Plan appears to be financially feasible though expensive at first. The main problem here is a political one, for, unlike the Qattara Depression which lies within the borders of one country, the shores of the Red Sea belong to different countries that are not always on the friendliest of political terms.

7. POWER FROM THE SUN

28. Eneas's solar power plant, South Pasadena, California, 1903

Power from the Sun

Many of the projects discussed in the preceding chapters have one thing in common, no matter how different they may be in details otherwise. There was always a point where the engineer said, "And here we can put a power dam," or, "The power plant will then be located at . . ." It might seem as if all the engineering projects for the future that do not deal with transportation are concerned with energy and power.

It not only seems that way; it is so.

The preoccupation of engineers with sources of power—"fuel" in any form or disguise—goes back to something that took place in 1913 and which, at first glance seemed to have little to do with any kind of engineering. In that year an International Geological Congress was held. Geologists from many countries met and told one another, and incidentally the world, of their discoveries. The formation and characteristics of some mountain chains had been learned. Maybe somebody read a paper on the Great Rift Valley.

Then one geologist reported on coal: how much was produced every year in the various countries, how production was likely to increase, and, most important, how much coal was probably still in the ground. All these factors added up to the problem of how long our coal supply could be expected to last.

At first the professor's words sounded rather reassuring. In all the coal seams likely to exist, down to a depth of 6000 feet below surface level, there could be expected to be enough coal for 5000 to 6000 years, at the rate at which coal was mined and used in 1913. Unfortunately this was merely a theoretical figure, for coal in the ground does not do anybody any good. To be useful it has to be mined and brought to the surface. But coal seams less than 28 inches in thickness cannot be mined, and even if a coal seam is thicker than this minimum figure a good portion of it stays in the ground for various reasons. Taking these facts into consideration, the "minable" coal would last only about 1500 years, still on the assumption that the rate of use stayed reasonably close to the 1913 rate.

Even under these assumptions the various countries did not fare equally well. It was then estimated that England would have coal for only about 200 years, Germany for 300 to 400 years. The United States came off best, with an estimated 2000 years.

Since these estimates were made, quite a number of things have happened. Most important, the yearly rate of coal production and coal consumption has been going up steadily. There have been two World Wars which squandered fuel of every kind. The over-all result is that the estimates of 1913 look unduly optimistic. The statistics which have been published from time to time unfortunately have a tendency to be confusing rather than enlightening. The figures run into so many million million tons of coal, plus so many million tons of oil, of oil from oil shale, of natural gas, and of tar, that they sound almost like the figures for the water budget of the Mediterranean Sea.[1]

---

[1] For example, in the United States alone the consumption of coal and other fuels during the year 1946 was as follows: coal, 583 million tons; oil, 1700 million

Engineers refer to all the fuels just named as "fossil fuels" because the coal and lignite and oil deposits are all the results of accumulations of once-living things, all of them plants. What is now a coal seam was 400 million years ago an enormous swampy forest where club mosses and horsetail rushes grew to the proportions of tall trees, intermixed with tree ferns and a whole list of other trees now completely extinct. If you throw a lump of coal on the fire you burn what is left of plants that were green and growing hundreds of millions of years ago; hence the term "fossil fuel." That term in itself implies the most significant fact: the fossil fuels cannot renew themselves. Once the supply of coal has been used up it is gone.

Another significant fact is that most coal-mining shafts in the United States are less than 1000 feet deep, while the *average* coal-mining shaft in England is more than 1000 feet deep. We can still afford to go deeper than we do now, but even so the coal fields in the so-called Eastern Province of the United States are not expected to last many more years. A few experts predict that these coal fields will become unproductive in only 90 years. Others are willing to grant 150 years. None dares to go higher.

It is true that oil supplies, especially in the United States, are expected to last much longer than the coal fields of the Eastern Province. Unexploited oil fields are known. However, if you add all the fossil fuels together, you find that coal accounts for a little more than 90 per cent of the total. Even if the oil supply should be doubled or tripled by the discovery of new and large fields, the over-all picture will not change greatly. What is actually more important is that engineers have learned to

---

barrels; natural gas, 4 million million cubic feet. It is easy to imagine the kind of figures one would get for worldwide consumption over a century or so.

obtain more useful energy from 1 ton of coal than their fathers obtained from 3 tons. Still, no matter how carefully we use a ton of coal nowadays, it is still a ton of coal, and the supply is limited. One day it will be exhausted.

That is the reason engineers are so much interested in new sources of energy. If a large power dam will cut the consumption of coal in half for a certain area the coal will obviously last twice as long. And the more time there is, the better founded are our hopes of finding a solution to the problem.

Interestingly enough, the chemical engineers encountered a somewhat similar problem at an earlier date. For various purposes large quantities of the element bromine were needed—far more than the normal production. The same was true of the metal magnesium. When these demands developed, it was already well known that both these elements occurred in the ocean, not in bottom deposits covered by ocean water, but dissolved in the ocean water itself. If the problem of extracting bromine and magnesium from ocean water could be solved, there could never again be a possibility of shortage, since the ocean would be a literally inexhaustible mine. The problem was solved, and if more magnesium and more bromine are needed, they can be had simply by building additional factories.

This experience looked like a pointer to the power engineers. They also knew of a literally inexhaustible source of energy: the energy which comes every day, year after year, from the sun. All they had to do was to find a way to trap and harness it.

To make the sun run a piece of machinery was not even a new idea; it had appeared in classical antiquity in the writings of Euclid, of Heron of Alexandria, and of Philon of Byzantium. The remarks of these classical writers are so unspecific that one can be quite certain that they did not describe things which had actually been built in their time but were merely throwing out ideas about things which ought to work. A curved mirror of large size was to concentrate the sun's rays on a spot or a small area. This would then produce air currents and the air currents could be used to run a windmill.

The first description of an actually working "solar motor" can be found in a book published in 1615.[2] Since the book contains a picture of the device it is quite certain that the little machine existed. A number of lenses, set in a wooden board, concentrated the sun's rays on airtight metal boxes which were partly filled with water. The air in the boxes expanded as it was heated and forced the water from the boxes; the water appeared in the form of a small indoor fountain in the next room. After sunset the air in the boxes would contract again and pull the water back in so that the machine was ready for use again the next morning. Another device, described in the same book, instead of making a small fountain play, operated a simple musical instrument. Of course these were just toys, but many technological developments have begun with things that either were designed as toys or were called toys by others.

Almost precisely two and a half centuries had to pass until the next step was taken. The man who took it was a French physics professor named Augustin Bernard Mouchot, who between 1864 and 1878 built a number of solar power plants which not only functioned but actually performed some work. Essentially Professor Mouchot's solar power plants were simple steam engines, except that the boiler was heated by the sun instead of by burning coal.

[2] *Les Raisons des forces movantes* by Salomon de Caus.

The sun's rays were collected by means of a rather large mirror which had very nearly the shape of an old-fashioned megaphone—in technical language, a truncated cone. The cone was tilted in such a way that its large opening pointed toward the sun. This would concentrate the sun's rays on the center line of the cone, where a tubular boiler was placed. The water in the boiler quickly changed to steam; the rest was more or less routine. Professor Mouchot started his solar boiler for the first time on September 22, 1864, near Algiers in North Africa; the steam engine coupled to the solar boiler drove a pump for irrigation purposes. Even Professor Mouchot's first unit was quite large; the largest diameter of the mirror was a full 5 meters (16.4 feet). The pump delivered 2½ tons of water per minute into the irrigation ditch.

Everyone praised Professor Mouchot for his ingenuity and wished him the best of luck. But years passed and nobody bought the engine. Mouchot thought he would surely find customers if only enough people could see his machine at work. Recognizing a wonderful opportunity in the Paris Exposition of 1878, he applied for space and built and displayed a machine of considerably larger dimensions than the one which had been used near Algiers. But there were no customers, for the very simple reason that a normal boiler with firebox was much cheaper and coal did not cost much.

What happened to Mouchot in Europe was repeated in precisely the same manner in the New World, except that here the story concerned a man who was already famous. He was John Ericsson, the inventor of the *Monitor*. Ericsson worked on solar power plants for a full ten years (1870–1880) but then gave up. Nobody seemed interested.

At the turn of the century it looked as if the pioneer work done by Mouchot and Ericsson had not been completely wasted. In 1901 one A. G. Eneas obtained a United States patent for a solar generator which resembled Mouchot's in general outline but had a number of additional features. For example, the mirror turned automatically in the course of the day so that it always pointed directly at the sun. In the following year such a generator was built and put to use on an ostrich farm at South Pasadena, California. The mirror had an opening of more than 30 feet; the tubular boiler in its center line held 150 gallons of water. One hour after sunrise the water had all been converted into steam and the 15-horsepower steam engine began to work. It drove pumps and a small generator.

The next name on the list of solar-engine inventors is that of Frank Shuman of Philadelphia, who began his work in about 1907. Shuman believed that the devices of Mouchot, Ericsson, and Eneas had suffered from being too expensive and that the main source of expense was the large mirror. At first he tried to do without any mirror at all, and when that did not turn out well he settled for flat mirrors which are far cheaper than curved mirrors. His "collectors" of solar heat were long troughs of metal, partly filled with water and covered by two glass panes to avoid heat losses. Long flat mirrors were mounted at a tilt on either side of the glass-covered boxes. The first model of such a power plant was built at Tacony, near Philadelphia, in 1911. It wasn't precisely a sensational success, but it was successful enough to attract some capital, and a firm with the name of Eastern Sun Power, Ltd., was founded.

An improved and enlarged version of the Tacony power plant was built by this company at Meadi in Egypt, about 10 miles south of Cairo. The "collectors" at the Meadi plant were long troughs like those at Tacony, but they had a different shape. The long mirrors were not flat but slightly curved, focusing the sun's rays in a line which ran the length of the trough some distance above the center of its bottom. The boilers were suspended on narrow rods along this focal line, all of them feeding their steam into a master steampipe which led to the steam engine.

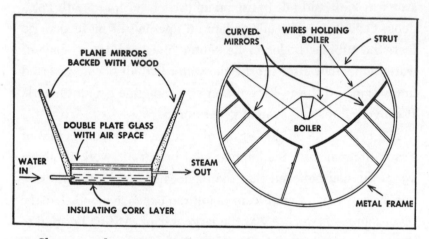

29. Shuman solar-energy collectors: (left) type used at Tacony, Pennsylvania; (right) type used at Meadi, Egypt

At first there were lots of difficulties. The boilers of the plant at Tacony had been made of sheet zinc which was simply soldered along the seams. At Meadi such boilers came apart and Eastern Sun Power, Ltd., finally had to make its boilers of sheet steel which was welded into shape. This was quite a novelty at the time but it worked, and by 1913 the wedge-shaped boilers were producing enough steam to feed a 100-horsepower low-pressure piston steam engine.

The purpose of the power plant was again irrigation, for Meadi

30. The solar power plant at Meadi, Egypt

is a cotton-growing district where the land is fertile provided it is watered. The irrigated area measured a total of 500 Egyptian *feddan* of cotton land. Since a *feddan* equals 45,200 square feet this was quite a large plantation.

The "over-all efficiency" of the machinery was about 5 per cent, which means that enough sunlight struck the mirrors to pump twenty times as much water as was actually pumped. The efficiency was so low because there were losses all along the line. To begin with, the mirrors did not reflect all the sun's rays into the boilers but absorbed some of them, heating up themselves. The boilers, instead of absorbing all the radiation they received, reflected some of it back. Next there were heat losses in the steam lines, and, finally, neither the steam engine nor the pumps worked without considerable losses. But in 1913 an over-all efficiency of 5 per cent was considered "not too bad"; many industrial establishments took such a low efficiency for granted. Besides, the energy was free, so why worry about losses as long as the thing worked? And it did work to the satisfaction of everybody concerned for several years; the power plant was finally permitted to fall into disuse at the end of the First World War.

After the First World War the center of solar power research shifted back to the United States, mostly because Dr. C. G. Abbot, long-time secretary and later president of the Smithsonian Institution, became an enthusiastic and untiring builder of solar power plants. In the course of several decades Dr. Abbot tried various types, his purpose being to see which type would serve best under a given set of conditions. Naturally the purpose for which a solar power plant is built is a very important factor; if you want only hot water the problem is different and as a rule much simpler than it is if you want steam to run an engine.

The simplest kind of solar water heater built by Dr. Abbot can be copied by anybody who lives in a climate with much sunshine and a normally cloudless sky. "While on Mount Wilson," Dr. Abbot wrote in his booklet *Utilizing Heat from the Sun,*[3] "I bought 200 feet of black garden hose. I coiled 150 feet of it in a flat coil upon a wooden X and carried it up the ladder to the south side of the cottage roof. The other 50 feet I connected to the water hydrant in the yard and to a spigot in the bathtub. By this simple arrangement we could draw 5 gallons of very hot water each half-hour on every sunny day."

Solar water heaters similar in principle to Dr. Abbot's are in daily use in Florida and other southern states. The most prevalent model consists of a shallow trough of blackened metal which is covered as tightly as possible with a glass pane. Inside this hot box there is something like a radiator of black metal pipes through which water is circulated. The hot water emerging from the device is then stored in an insulated container. If all parts are well protected against heat losses by heavy insulation there will be hot water for household use any time, day or night.

Other solar engines built by Dr. Abbot bore a greater resemblance to the power plant at Meadi. They consisted of one or several curved trough mirrors with boilers in their focal lines. But there were also a number of important differences. At Meadi the solar collectors had been parallel to the ground. True, a mechanism made them follow the sun so that one half of the

[3] Smithsonian Miscellaneous Collections, vol. 98, no. 8, 1939.

mirror would never shade the other half. But since they were flat on the ground the sun would still shine slantwise into the troughs to a greater or less degree all the time.

To get the maximum of sunlight into the device the tubular boiler and the line from its middle to the sun should form an inverted T. This may sound difficult to accomplish but is actually quite easy, especially since astronomers solved a similar problem for mounting their telescopes centuries ago. All that needs to be done is to raise one end of the assembly so that the axis of the boiler points in the direction of the North Star. If it does that, the boiler is parallel to the axis of the earth; then it is necessary only to turn the mirror on its tilted axis at the rate of 15 degrees of arc per hour and the sun will always shine into the mirror (see fig. 31) with a minimum of loss.

Another important difference between Dr. Abbot's devices and the Meadi power plant was that he did not use water in his boiler. At first he filled the system with ordinary engine oil, but he found that it had some disadvantages. It tended to char the inside of the tubes and it began to evaporate at 400 degrees Fahrenheit. Therefore Dr. Abbot substituted a chemical named Arochlor for the oil. It is a nearly black liquid, which absorbs heat well because of its color, does not boil until heated to 665 degrees Fahrenheit, and does not evaporate much at temperatures below its boiling point. As a matter of fact, Dr. Abbot did not want it to boil; he just wanted a lot of very hot oil, which was then fed into an insulated jacket around an oven. Dr. Abbot actually baked biscuits and small cakes in such ovens, which reached and maintained a temperature of about 265 degrees Fahrenheit. This would not be hot enough for broiling meat, but it is hot enough for baking and for dishes which have to simmer

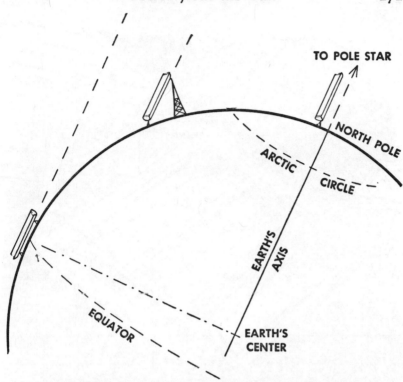

TO POLE STAR

NORTH POLE

ARCTIC CIRCLE

EARTH'S AXIS

EQUATOR

EARTH'S CENTER

31. Principle of telescope-like mounting of a solar collector

slowly for a long time. It is also hot enough to distill sea water into drinking water, but for this specific purpose another type of solar heater was built.

In 1933 the Russians built a small experimental power plant in Tashkent, the capital of the Uzbek Soviet Republic, and announced that they would follow up with one large enough to supply the whole city. The large power plant never materialized. The small one, which operated a kitchen and a bath, seems to have been constructed along the lines of Dr. Abbot's experimental units.

While Dr. Abbot wanted fairly low temperatures for such

32. One of Dr. Abbot's solar collectors

purposes as hot water for household uses and enough heat for
baking, the French engineer Felix Trombe has gone to the opposite extreme. He has built a solar engine of a rather spectacu-
lar kind high up in the mountains on the French side of the
Pyrenees. The foundations for his power plant are the heavy
walls of a 300-year-old fortress called Montlouis. Felix Trombe
works with an arrangement consisting of two large compound
mirrors. One is the concentrating mirror, made of a paraboloid
metal shell 31 feet in diameter, on which 3500 small plane mirrors are mounted. This concentrating mirror is stationary; it

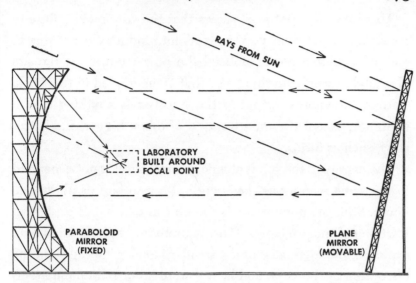

33. Principle of the French solar laboratory in the Pyrenees

would catch the sun's rays not much more than 2 hours a day even if it faced due south, which it does not. To make it work for most of the day it has been built facing north to receive the sun's rays at second hand from a flat mirror some 80 feet away. The flat mirror, measuring 43 by 34 feet and composed of 516 plate-glass mirrors, follows the sun and reflects the rays into the paraboloid concentrating mirror. The focal point is naturally on the line between the two mirrors and a research laboratory has been built around the focal point (fig. 33). The smallest area upon which the sun's rays can be concentrated is about 4 inches in diameter; the temperature is 5400 degrees Fahrenheit, enough literally to burn bricks and to melt a hole in a piece of armor plate in less than half a minute. The quantity of heat collected is enormous too; the mirror assembly can melt 130 pounds of iron per hour!

This experiment at least shows that the continued failure of inventors to put solar power plants into industry is not due to lack of available power. Indeed the power output of the sun absolutely dwarfs anything else that is mentioned in this book. Rather, the energy output of the sun dwarfs anything else in existence, except the energy output of other, bigger, and hotter stars, such as Sirius.

The energy of the sun is atomic energy, but it is not generated in the same manner as the energy of a uranium or plutonium bomb. Still, the normal atomic bomb can be used to explain at least one of the principles. When a uranium or plutonium bomb explodes, the total mass of the smaller atoms resulting from the disruption of the large and heavy uranium or plutonium atoms does not quite add up to the original mass. The missing portion, which is quite small, appears as energy. Similarly, the helium which is the result of the explosion of a hydrogen bomb has a slightly smaller mass than the hydrogen before the explosion. Again the missing portion appears as energy.

The sun operates along the lines of the hydrogen bomb. Deep in its interior, where the pressures are high and the temperatures enormous, hydrogen atoms are steadily being fused into helium atoms. Although this has been going on for at least 5000 million years the sun still has a very abundant hydrogen supply. In fact, the sun still consists mostly of hydrogen; the best available estimate says that there are twelve times as many hydrogen atoms in the sun as all other atoms taken together. This supply will last the sun for at least another 5000 million years, even though 564 million tons of hydrogen are converted into 560 million tons of helium every second. In other words, 4 million tons of matter are destroyed every second, to appear as light and other radiations of all kinds.

In the hydrogen bomb, where the hydrogen to be fused probably weighs less than 100 pounds, the process of fusion is incredibly fast; in the sun, where millions of tons of matter are involved, it looks slow and steady. Nor are the two processes precisely the same—in the bomb the fusion seems to take place directly and all at once; in the sun the process goes through several successive stages. One possible pattern that is being followed was discovered independently in 1938 by two scientists, Dr. Hans Bethe in the United States and Dr. Carl von Weizsäcker in Germany.

What happens is this: A carbon atom of mass 12—this means that it is twelve times as massive as a single hydrogen atom—receives a hydrogen atom, or, to be precise, the nucleus of a hydrogen atom.[4] When the nucleus of the atom of carbon-12 and the hydrogen nucleus combine they form the nucleus of an atom of nitrogen of mass 13, giving off a burst of gamma rays as a by-product. Gamma rays, like all other rays, are a form of energy. In this first stage of the six-stage process, one hydrogen atom disappears and some radiation, or energy, is liberated.

The second stage is caused by the fact that a nitrogen-13 nucleus is not stable; it cannot last, and in order to stabilize itself it throws out a subatomic particle called a positron. The positron itself is so small that its loss does not noticeably change the mass of the nucleus. But the chemical nature of the atom is changed;

[4] Here on earth a single electron would revolve around that hydrogen nucleus, but in the hot interior of the sun the electrons are normally stripped off so that the interplay of reactions takes place between nuclei of atoms rather than between "complete" atoms.

it is now no longer nitrogen of mass 13 but carbon of mass 13.

In the third stage the carbon-13 nucleus receives another hydrogen nucleus; emitting another burst of gamma rays, they unite into a nitrogen nucleus of mass 14.

This nitrogen-14 nucleus, as the fourth stage of the process, takes another hydrogen nucleus unto itself to form an oxygen-atom nucleus of mass 15, as usual giving off a burst of gamma rays.

Like the nitrogen-13 nucleus, the oxygen-15 nucleus is not stable. It throws out a positron and changes into nitrogen-15. That is the fifth stage.

The sixth and last stage is that the nitrogen-15 nucleus absorbs the fourth hydrogen atom that is used up in the process. The result this time, however, is different from those of the earlier steps. In all the earlier stages, either two fused atoms made another atom, accompanied by a release of energy, or else one atom changed into another atom. From the sixth stage, two different atoms result. One is a helium atom, or rather its nucleus, which is also called an "alpha particle." The other is a carbon nucleus of mass 12, the same type of carbon atom with which the whole process started, ready to do it all over again, as long as hydrogen atoms are available.[5]

---

[5] It is easier to follow what happens if you write this down in a somewhat tabulated form, with the letters H, O, C, and N standing for hydrogen, oxygen, carbon, and nitrogen:

First step	C-12 + H-1	makes	N-13, plus gamma rays
Second step	N-13	becomes	C-13 by losing positron
Third step	C-13 + H-1	makes	N-14, plus gamma rays
Fourth step	N-14 + H-1	makes	O-15, plus gamma rays
Fifth step	O-15	becomes	N-15 by losing positron
Sixth step	N-15 + H-1	makes	He-4 (helium-4) and C-12

Over-all result: four hydrogen atoms have disappeared, a helium atom has been made, energy has been released, and carbon 12 starts over again.

In classical times there was a legend of a wonderful bird, the phoenix, of which only one specimen was alive at a time. At the end of its lifespan of 500 years, the story went, the phoenix built a nest and laid one egg. Then it set the nest afire. The old phoenix died in the flames, but the heat of the fire hatched the egg and the new phoenix rose into the air. Because that carbon-12 atom appears, like the legendary phoenix, unchanged out of the atomic fire of its own making, this six-stage cycle has been called the Solar Phoenix Reaction. At first it was believed that virtually all the energy produced by our sun came from this particular fusion reaction. But then Critchfield calculated another five-step reaction which is called the H-H process, also converting hydrogen into helium but at a slower rate. Between them the carbon cycle and the H-H process liberate the energy which the sun radiates into space. All other atomic reactions produce far more or else far less energy than is actually observed.

The total energy output of the sun is another one of those incredible figures. If our sun were the heat source of an engine built by a race of supercosmic giants whose engines not only are of colossal size but also operate with 100-per-cent efficiency, it would deliver 500,000,000,000,000,000,000,000,000 horsepower, or 500,000 million million million horsepower.

Naturally this represents radiation over the whole globe of the sun. The earth receives only a tiny portion of the total. Being 93 million miles from the sun and just about 7900 miles in diameter, the earth intercepts very little indeed, not quite one two-thousandth of a millionth part of what the sun throws into space. Even that little is much; it could melt, in the course of a year, a uniform layer of ice 115 feet thick over the whole earth. Compared to fossil fuel, the energy intercepted by our planet every single second is worth 6 million tons of coal.

To reduce all this to figures small enough to be grasped, let's consider just a single acre of area. If the earth had no atmosphere, with the sun vertically overhead, that single acre would receive 7400 horsepower worth of solar energy. As it is, *if* the sky is cloudless without any mists or duststorms, that acre will receive the equivalent of 5000 horsepower; the difference goes into heating the air in between. Solar collectors like those of Shuman and Abbot require space between them so that they will not shade each other in the early morning and late afternoon hours. Two-thirds of the acre will thus be unoccupied; the remaining third receives 1666 horsepower. Then there are unavoidable losses, since the mirrors do not reflect, or the boilers absorb, everything they get; the working fluid in the boilers can be expected to absorb 555 horsepower worth of solar energy. After conversion of the heat in the fluid into useful power 83 horsepower per acre is left; in reality it is probably nearer 50 horsepower.

An actual yield of 50 horsepower per acre is still a very nice figure. Unfortunately this nice figure is achieved only part of the time, when the sky is really cloudless. The French say that their solar energy research station in the Pyrenees has 250 such days per year and the engineers at Meadi counted on 300 days per year. Cloudless skies seem to be the rule at Meadi; the French station can count on its high figure mostly for the reason that it is far above sea level and most of the clouds are below. In both places one can apparently count on a cloudless sky for the whole day if the day dawns cloudlessly. Elsewhere the situation is less satisfactory by far.

At the Massachusetts Institute of Technology, where several

solar research programs have been running for a number of years, care was taken to tabulate the number of hours of sunshine per day for half a dozen typical localities. This tabulation looks as follows:

SUNSHINE

PLACE	WINTER	SUMMER
Boston, Mass.	4.9 hours or 51 per cent	9.0 hours or 61 per cent
New York, N.Y.	5.5 hours or 56 per cent	9.7 hours or 67 per cent
Miami, Fla.	7.6 hours or 70 per cent	8.8 hours or 65 per cent
Chicago, Ill.	4.3 hours or 44 per cent	10.7 hours or 70 per cent
Los Angeles, Calif.	7.4 hours or 72 per cent	10.5 hours or 75 per cent
Seattle, Wash.	2.6 hours or 29 per cent	9.4 hours or 62 per cent

The percentage figures following the number of hours of sunshine indicate the relationship of actual sunshine to the amount of sunshine possible for the geographical latitude of the place named at the given season. In Boston, in winter, for example, the sun "shone" only half the time it was in the sky. Los Angeles in summer had sunshine only three-quarters of the possible time. In short, although the amount of energy available from the sun is theoretically more than we'll ever need, places in the temperate zone do not receive as much as one would expect.

When we try to draw conclusions from these facts we soon find that we must first consider the purpose for which the solar heat is intended. If the purpose is household use, the picture not only differs from but virtually contrasts with the one we get if we are considering solar energy for industrial purposes. As far as household use is concerned, it is evident that much fossil fuel can be saved in large areas of the United States. If a solar heater on the roof manufactures the hot water needed for laundry and bathing on 200 days per year, fuel need be expended for such purposes on only 165 days. Or if the living space of a house is kept warm by means of big picture windows which trap solar energy neatly, fuel can be used only for the cloudy days and during the nights. There is no doubt that solar energy, trapped for household purposes, can prolong the supply of fossil fuels.

But when it comes to industrial use, not only is the prospect fairly hopeless, but the picture acquires a number of decidedly silly aspects. The first stumbling block is what technologists call the "intermittence of supply." In plain language, this means what everybody knows anyway: that since the sun does not shine at night, power can be obtained only during the day. For some purposes that does not matter. It is no accident that the three installations which did useful work, Professor Mouchot's power plant near Algiers, Eneas's engine at South Pasadena, and the Meadi power station, were all used for irrigation. That is one of the cases where intermittence can easily be accepted. In most cases, unfortunately, intermittence is not acceptable. Even if a manufacturing plant had carefully adapted its operations to intermittence there are still cloudy days—and in the tropics whole rainy seasons—to spoil the organizational timetable. I can't imagine a factory that could function at all—not to mention making a profit—if, at irregular intervals, it had to attach a sign to its gate, saying: "Sorry, no power today. The Weather Bureau says it will clear up by Wednesday. Please report for work then." Such a factory would need "stand-by power" from a coal pile or an oil tank. But stand-by power, or rather the machinery which produces it, costs money, and the factory designer would greatly prefer "firm power," as supplied, for example, by a waterfall.

The sun delivers "firm power" only in space. Below the atmosphere on the turning earth the delivery is dubious. Just where it would be welcomed most, in the northern parts of the settled continents and during the winter, the smallest amount is received. Even in the southern parts of the settled continents, as in Europe south of the Alps and in the southern United States, the unreliability of delivery and reception is still too high to be acceptable. The only logical place to harness the sun, accepting intermittence, is in the deserts. But there very little power is needed, since most people have the good sense to live elsewhere.

The problem of utilizing solar energy for industry is clearly a twofold problem. Collecting and converting the energy is its first aspect, storing it is the second; and this second aspect is more important and certainly more difficult than the first.

None of the various methods for collecting the energy is good enough right now, although improvement may be possible. Only the mirror-type collectors have been described, because they are the best so far, in spite of all their shortcomings. But there are some other ways and means of converting solar energy into electric current directly, without mirrors, boilers, and steam engines. Best known are the thermocouple and the photoelectric cell, also called the "electric eye." A thermocouple is simply a wire loop, the two halves of the loop consisting of two different metals. The "classical" thermocouple is made of zinc and antimony soldered together. If one of the two joints is heated and the other kept cool a faint electric current will appear in the wire, but the average efficiency is 0.5 per cent. Dr. Maria Telkes, working at M.I.T., has designed thermocouples consisting of lead sulfide and zinc antimonide, which achieved an efficiency of 5 per cent.

This is certainly a record in its field, but it is not enough. To be useful the efficiency of the thermocouple should be at least 20 per cent. The two questions coming up after this statement are both unanswered. They are: Are such high efficiency thermocouples possible? And if they are, what will they cost?

The thermocouple operates on heat, the photoelectric cell on light. A good photoelectric cell, producing electric current when exposed to light, also has an efficiency of 0.5 per cent. Everything else that may be said about it has already been said with regard to thermocouples.

Another device, developed in about 1952, is the "solar battery" (also called "silicon cell") which has already seen wide application as a power source for the transmitters of artificial satellites. It resembles the older photoelectric cells in that it is operated by the sun's light rather than by its heat. A solar battery consists of a large number of thin wafers of silicon, each about the size of two razor blades laid end to end, and no thicker. The silicon is refined to an incredible extent: it has been stated that in every ten million atoms only one is an atom of a different kind; all the others are silicon. Next the silicon wafers are treated by heating them in the presence of another element or substance the nature of which has so far not been disclosed. The treated wafers, when struck by sunlight, become electrically charged, positive on the outside and negative in their interior. The rest is easy. The current is drained off by two fine wires, one attached to the surface and the other to the interior, and the wires from a large number of such wafers are connected up as if the wafers were so many tiny batteries—which, in effect, they are.

Naturally the solar battery will work only for as long as there is sunlight. But while the sun is shining, 6 per cent of the light that falls on the battery is converted into current, and in some units the efficiency has been doubled. Theoretically the device should never wear out or even become weaker; to learn what happens in practice, such batteries are being used as power supplies for rural telephone lines.

Researchers have come up with a third method: a kind of chemical cell. The chemicals in these cells change under the influence of sunlight; you might say that they soak up energy which they release again in the dark. This sounds intriguing in spite of a very low efficiency, for one is likely to jump to the conclusion that such cells, when improved, might be a method for storing and shipping solar energy. It must have occurred to everybody who ever thought about the problem that all the difficulties would disappear if one could ship the energy. Then a power plant could be located in a hot and sunny desert without regard to a lack of customers nearby. Unfortunately the reversal in the chemical cells begins as soon as the light source fails. They cannot be crated up and shipped without losing whatever energy they have temporarily stored.

How about making electricity and shipping that?

Contrary to a widespread and firmly held belief, electricity is not a form of energy that lends itself to being transported easily. For various reasons, transportation by means of high-voltage wires becomes impracticable if the distance is too long, say, more than 500 miles. And the only other known method, the accumulator—the "battery" of the family car—is a very poor one. True, you can get out again a large percentage of the current that is put into the accumulator, but you cannot put in much. Storage batteries are enormously heavy for the small quantity of electricity they are able to absorb. If you imagine a man pasting a square inch of wallpaper on a door and then transporting the door for the sake of the square inch of wallpaper which is needed at the other end of the trip, you have about the right idea of what it means to ship electricity by storage battery.

If one day somebody invents a really workable method of storing electricity, the problem of utilizing solar energy for industry will have to be re-examined.

In the meantime we'll have to be content with the knowledge that, in case of extreme need, there would indeed be a way of storing and shipping the energy collected by a solar power plant. This method—workable but expensive—operates by converting the energy into a fuel that can be shipped, namely, gasoline and similar chemical fuels. To do this three raw materials are needed, all of them inexhaustible. They are sunshine, water, and carbon dioxide from the air; the last-named will be returned automatically to the atmosphere as the fuel is used.

Making gasoline out of sunshine is a procedure requiring three major steps along with the three basic raw materials. Step no. 1 would be the familiar one of converting sunshine into electric current by means of collectors, boilers, and generators. Step no. 2 would be the use of the electric current for decomposing water into its two constituent elements, hydrogen and oxygen. Step no. 3 would be the conversion of the hydrogen into the substances known to chemists as hydrocarbons (gasoline is one of them), taking the carbon from the carbon dioxide of the air. Pure oxygen in large quantities might be trapped as a salable byproduct.

Most of the difficulty lies in the third step, and the main reason for the difficulties is that there is so little carbon dioxide in the atmosphere— only 0.03 per cent of the total. Since the known industrial chemical processes resulting in hydrocarbons require reasonably pure carbon dioxide to work well, it is first necessary to concentrate it out of the air. This is not really difficult, merely tedious and expensive. One could, for example, liquefy the air; at the temperature at which nitrogen and oxygen are liquids, carbon dioxide is a solid, the well-known "dry ice" of commerce. Or—a method which is probably easier to handle and also cheaper—one could fall back on two well-known household chemicals. If air is bubbled through a solution of caustic soda, the carbon dioxide will be absorbed and sodium bicarbonate will be formed. The sodium-bicarbonate solution can be decomposed by electric current, producing pure carbon dioxide and returning the caustic soda to the solution.

Doesn't sound too hard? No, but because the carbon-dioxide content of the air near the ground is only 0.03 per cent (carbon dioxide is virtually absent higher up), a million cubic feet of air must be processed for every gallon of gasoline produced. This would raise the price per gallon to about $3.00 at the chemical plant, and if the gasoline is shipped the price goes still higher, for the shipping itself costs fuel. By ordinary gasoline truck, for example, it costs 1 gallon to transport 20 tons 1 mile, which means that after a trip of 2000 miles only half the gasoline originally loaded is still there. Barring airlift, that is the most expensive method. A Diesel truck will transport 80 tons 1 mile per gallon of fuel consumed. Transport by railroad tank cars is slightly less expensive, but in a pipeline 1 gallon of fuel (for pumps, etc.) will transport 1090 tons 1 mile. And a sea-going tanker can carry 2360 tons 1 mile per gallon of fuel.

Still, such gasoline costs too much even at the plant, as long as there are fossil fuels available. Just as our earlier reasoning ended with "if somebody invents a really workable method of storing electricity," so the present line of reasoning ends on a similar note: the project will become more feasible, if somebody finds a way of utilizing the atmospheric carbon dioxide without need for separation and concentration.

At this point the agricultural expert enters the solar-energy debate to point out that it is not necessary to invent something which operates on sunlight and utilizes the atmospheric carbon dioxide without concentration. Such a thing is known. It is the living plant. Says the agriculturist, you don't have to build solar collectors and power stations and chemical plants to manufacture fuel. All you have to do is to plant real plants and grow your fuel. Not forests for firewood; wood is useful for making things but for fuel a forest grows too slowly. If you want to grow fuel, grow corn or potatoes, or, if the soil and climate permit, sugar cane. Or, best of all, grow sugar beets, which produce a bigger crop per acre than any of the others mentioned, three times as much as corn or potatoes and even more than sugar cane. The fuel that can be derived from any and all of these crops is alcohol, a very fine liquid fuel, not quite as good as gasoline for existing engines but better than anything else.

As technology now stands the agricultural expert is right: the best and simplest way of harnessing solar energy is by way of the living plant. If our fossil fuels gave out within the next decade agricultural alcohol would have to save the day. But the fossil fuels will last for a century—and nobody can predict what may be invented in the meantime.

8. WAVES AND WARM WATER

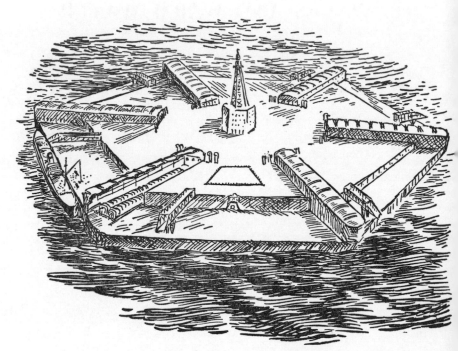

34. A floating island as a power plant utilizing the difference in temperature between surface and bottom water.

Waves and Warm Water

Not quite twenty-five centuries ago an army of Greeks embarked on a campaign against the Persian king Artaxerxes II. The campaign ended badly; near an ancient city called Cunaxa the leader of the Greeks lost his life, many of his officers were murdered by the Persians, and the army found itself leaderless 1000 miles from home, then an incredible distance. They might never have made it back, or we might know little about it if they had, had it not been for a Greek nobleman who was present. He was elected an officer and led the army back. The new leader, whose name was Xenophon, also happened to be an exceptionally gifted writer and for this reason we have a complete account of the whole campaign.

When the Greeks finally neared the end of their 1000-mile march, the hills opened up and blue showed below the horizon. The soldiers greeted the sight with joyous shouts of *"Thalatta, thalatta!"* ("The sea, the sea!") All the relief they felt after the long march of despair was expressed in that one shout. They saw the sea and felt that they were saved.

The story told by Xenophon may apply to modern man as well. Marching along the road of diminishing supplies, with ever greater need for them, modern man also looks at the seas which are bounded by nothing but the horizon. *Thalatta, thalatta*—the sea may save us too.

That the seas are an inexhaustible mine of chemicals and metals has been mentioned. From sea water we extract bromine and quantities of magnesium metal. We know that a cubic mile of sea water holds 12,000 million pounds of magnesium. Sea water also holds per cubic mile 18,000 pounds of uranium, tons of gold, and many tons of iron, and even rare metals like praseodymium in larger amounts than have ever been produced from all other sources. All that we need to do is to find efficient methods of recovery, if, as, and when this becomes necessary. So far we have tapped the mineral resources of the sea only to the extent we have touched its food resources, which is like gathering a bucketful of seeds from a large field of grain.

Engineers and physicists in their quest for new energy sources have looked at the seas too, and more than one has shouted *"Thalatta"* and announced that all our energy troubles can be cured by harnessing the wind-swept ocean.

The seas offer energy not in just one form but in at least four different forms: the waves, the surf, the tides, and finally—something a layman may not think of at once—the difference in temperature between the waters of the ocean's surface and the deep layers.

When it comes to harnessing either the seas or the winds, the reasoning is similar to that we met in the discussion of solar energy. Wind and waves are proverbially unreliable. There are coastlines where there is always some surf, but the surf may be destructively heavy today and gentle tomorrow. The tides are intermittent, if at least predictable. But the difference of the temperatures of surface water and of the deep layers promises "firm power."

Of course even the warmest surface water of a tropical sea is still far below boiling point, and one cannot hope to extract energy from it by means of a regular steam engine. But there are "steam engines" in which the steam used is not water vapor but the vapor of another liquid with a far different boiling point. In some industrial plants, especially power plants, the working fluid in boilers and turbines is metallic mercury, which boils under normal pressure at a temperature of 674.5 degrees Fahrenheit. A mercury-vapor engine, therefore, works at a much higher temperature than a water-vapor engine. A likely working fluid for a low-temperature engine is sulfur dioxide, which is normally known only as a vapor. It is the sharp-smelling gas that forms when sulfur is burned, but it becomes a gas only at temperatures above 17 degrees Fahrenheit.

What counts for power generation is not the highest temperature available but the difference in temperatures that can be obtained in a given place. This has been called the temperature-level difference, in direct comparison to a waterfall, and just as one waterfall has a high drop while another has only a low one, so the difference in temperature levels may be large or small. In general, our engines work with rather big level differences of several hundred degrees, but this does not mean that no other engines are possible.

Probably the first to consider the extraction of energy from small temperature-level differences was the French physicist, Professor Jacques Arsène d'Arsonval. An article by him about this problem appeared in the French scientific magazine *Revue scientifique*, in the issue of September 17, 1881. He used a warm spring in France, the Spring of Grenelle, as his first example. The temperature of that spring is 86 degrees Fahrenheit; the average temperature of river water nearby is 60 degrees Fahrenheit. If one placed a boiler in the spring and cooled the condenser of the steam engine with river water the temperature difference between boiler and condenser would be 26 degrees Fahrenheit. If the boiler were filled with liquid sulfur dioxide, d'Arsonval wrote, it would be quickly vaporized and develop a noticeable pressure, and the difference in vapor pressure between boiler and condenser would be enough to drive an engine of some kind without any expense other than the initial cost and maintenance.

Although, Professor d'Arsonval continued, there are lots of warm springs all over the earth, these are by no means the only localities which favor such a scheme. The engine would work if the boiler were in normal "cold" river water and the condenser in a glacier. Ideally, d'Arsonval wrote (no doubt smiling as he did so), the boiler should be in the ocean at the equator and the condenser in the ice of Greenland's interior. But one can get the same effect in any deep spot of the warm seas, for the bottom water of the ocean, even under the equator, is never warmer than 39 to 41 degrees Fahrenheit, so that a boiler at the surface and a condenser a mile below should do the trick.

Most people who read d'Arsonval's article considered this an amusing as well as a novel idea, correct in theory too, no doubt, but of no practical importance. That, remember, was in 1881.

After the report on the probable supplies of fossil fuels at the Geological Congress of 1913, several men grew thoughtful and began to work on the same problem. Some of them may have had the same idea independently; others knew about d'Arsonval's article, especially since in the meantime he had become very famous as an electrical researcher. One of the first to publish his investigations (in 1913) was an American, William Campbell; he was followed by two Italians, Dornig and Boggia, and one German, the physicist Dr. E. Bräuer. All of them were much more thorough and detailed than d'Arsonval, who had merely broken ground. But none of them succeeded in attracting much attention.

This general indifference suddenly disappeared in November 1926, when the French Academy of Sciences received a report signed with two names: Georges Claude and Paul Boucherot. Boucherot was known chiefly as an associate and collaborator of Claude's, but Claude was well known for a number of things. He had invented a method for transporting acetylene safely. He was one of the originators of the modern method of liquefying air. He had acquired fame for his work on the rare gases and he had invented the neon tube which changed the appearance of all large cities. In the course of all this he had also become a wealthy man, a fact which became important when he began to experiment with the extraction of energy by means of small temperature-level difference.

Claude and Boucherot began their report by stating the well-known fact that the water at the surface of a tropical sea has a temperature between 78 and 85 degrees Fahrenheit, while the bottom water in the same spot registers on a thermometer with about 39 to 41 degrees. They went on to say that it would be easy to bring the cold bottom water close to the warm surface water by means of a well-insulated pipe. Since the bottom water has a slightly higher specific gravity it would not rise to the actual surface in the insulated pipe. Its level in the pipe would be about 3 or 4 feet below the level of the warm surface water, so that pumps would be needed to bridge this very short distance.

"Mostly out of curiosity and not because we harbored great hopes," the report continued, the two scientists tried whether a temperature difference of only 50 degrees Fahrenheit could be made to do work. They filled a large glass bottle partly full of water of a temperature of 82 degrees Fahrenheit and led the low-pressure water vapor through a glass pipe into a small turbine wheel. This turbine wheel was in another large glass bottle, the bottom of which was covered with a layer of crushed ice. To start the apparatus, an air pump, connected with the neck of the second bottle, had to evacuate the air from both bottles until the pressure had been reduced to the point at which the warm water began to boil. From then on the little experimental machine ran by itself, the spent steam condensing around the crushed ice to form water and the turbine driving a small dynamo which supplied current to three small electric bulbs.

The steam pressure in the boiler (the first bottle) was a mere 3 per cent of ordinary atmospheric pressure—so low that the walls of the glass bottle were strained in the "wrong direction." The danger was not that the bottle might explode but that it might implode, that is, be crushed by the atmospheric pressure.

After this little laboratory experiment Paul Boucherot, the engineer of the team, designed a fairly large unit which was tested in Belgium by utilizing the cooling water of the blast furnaces of Ougrée-Marihaye. The cold condenser water was furnished by the river Meuse, and if the water coming from the blast furnaces happened to be too cold some steam was led into it so that its temperature was always 36 degrees Fahrenheit higher than that of the river. This temperature difference is less than can be expected in a tropical sea, but the reasoning probably was that if the machine would run on a difference of 36 degrees Fahrenheit, it would certainly run on the difference of 50 degrees which could be expected in the Caribbean Sea. The "pilot plant" was ready April 25, 1928, and was tested for the first time on April 29. It worked. Of course the system required all kinds of auxiliary machinery, especially air pumps, all of which used electric current. The first measurements were made to find out how much of the current generated was eaten up by the auxiliary equipment. The result sounded hopeful indeed: only 25 per cent of the total output was needed to keep the whole running.

Claude and Boucherot then invited the Academy of Science to send a commission to inspect their pilot plant. The commission arrived on June 1, 1928. Its spokesman, Professor Le Chatelier, wrote a careful and, in general, rather friendly report. The machine works, he said, and Monsieur Claude has thereby proved his first point; the second point, which still remains to be demonstrated, is whether a mile-long insulated pipe can be constructed and used to obtain cold bottom water from an ocean.

Claude, being rich and enthusiastic, quickly decided to use his own money to transport the pilot plant in Belgium (also paid for out of his own pocket) to a suitable place in the tropics. For the sake of simplicity, and also to reduce expenses, the plant was to be erected at a seashore where the three essential conditions were fulfilled. The first of these conditions was location in the tropics, for the sake of warm surface water. The second was that the shoreline should drop quickly to great depths, so that the cold-water pipe did not have to have excessive length. And the third was a reasonably strong ocean current near the shore so that the "used water," of intermediate temperature, would be swept away quickly. After a considerable number of studies, the bay of Matanzas on the north shore of Cuba, some 50 miles east of Havana, was picked.

The sea there is between 82 and 83 degrees Fahrenheit, about as warm as a tropical sea can be. There is also a current which would remove the mixed water. The only thing that was not ideal was the incline of the sea bottom. It did not go down as steeply as would have been desirable, and the cold-water pipe had to be 1.2 miles long. For the immediate purpose of running the pilot plant the cold-water pipe would not have needed a diameter greater than 18 or 20 inches, but since Claude wanted to use it for a later and much bigger power plant he made the pipe large, with a diameter of nearly 5 feet. It was made of sheet steel in 60-foot sections and insulated. A 500-foot section was pushed out from the shore; the main portion was laid on the sea bottom. Divers were supposed to connect the main portion to the shore piece, which, at its extreme end, was about 60 feet below the surface.

This sounded like an arrangement which should avoid all mishaps, but Claude was in for a streak of bad luck. The first pipe was lost because the ropes broke and the pipe came to rest on the sea bottom too far down for divers to work. The second pipe, in the course of operations, received a bad kink and developed a long leak which could not be repaired. At the third try (September 7, 1930) things at long last went as planned, but unfortunately the pipe was comparatively short, ending at a depth of only 2000 feet below the surface. On October 1, 1930, the machine ran for the first time. In Belgium it had been a 50-kilowatt unit; in Cuba it produced a mere 22 kilowatts. The main reason was that the water from 2000 feet was not cold enough. It arrived at the condensers with a temperature of 58 degrees Fahrenheit so that the all-important temperature difference, instead of being 50 degrees as was to be expected, or even

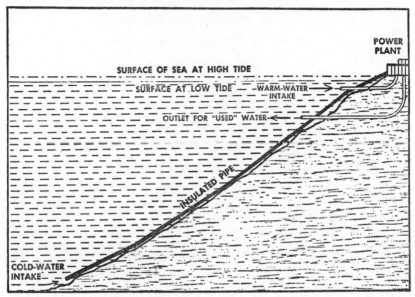

35. A Claude power plant, shore-based as in the Bay of Matanzas

36 degrees, as in Belgium, was only 24 degrees. To make things look even worse than they were, the pump for the 5-foot-wide cold-water pipe was far too powerful. It required more current than the plant produced; Claude had to buy current from the Cuban power companies.

Claude and Boucherot both saw that the demonstration at the bay of Matanzas was anything but impressive, and the experiment was discontinued. But they both felt satisfied that the important point had been proved; their machine *had* run on ocean water. That it had performed poorly was due to secondary circumstances which could be corrected.

Claude's idea of how his power plant would look when finished had been something quite different from a seashore station. He had visualized a floating island, almost like Armstrong's floating islands (Chapter 2), but of different shape and for a different purpose. Claude's final power plant was to be a hexagonal floating island, with a diameter of 2000 feet. In the center there was to be a small lighthouse to indicate its position to ships and to aircraft. Six powerhouses were to radiate from the center to the corners of the hexagon, each with four sets of turbogenerators with an output of 40,000 kilowatts each. This made 160,000 kilowatts per powerhouse or close to a million kilowatts for the whole island. The warm water was to be taken in through the bottom of the island, the cold water through a freely hanging vertical pipe 2000 to 3000 feet long, while the mixed water was to be discharged at a depth of 300 or 400 feet. Claude did not want to store the current as current; it was to be used to make commercial chemicals which could be shipped by freighter. Although he did not say so specifically he was probably thinking of extraction of chemicals and metals from sea water, a process which at that time was still in the dream stage itself.

Partly because of the final shape they had in mind, partly because they put all the blame for the Cuban misadventure on the difficulties of having a very long pipe rest on the ocean floor, Claude and Boucherot decided on a ship-borne unit as the next step. A 10,000-ton steamer, the *Tunisie,* was equipped with an 800-kilowatt set of the same design as the original pilot plant.

The all-important cold-water pipe was redesigned. A 200-ton block of solid concrete formed the anchor to which the lower end of the pipe was literally chained, leaving ample space between the concrete and the end of the pipe for the water to enter. At the upper end of the pipe there was a spherical float which by its high buoyancy held the pipe as nearly vertical as sea currents would permit. The spherical float and the upper end of the pipe were 50 feet below the surface, so that in bad weather the steamer could disconnect and abandon the pipe temporarily until the storm had passed.

All this was quite ingenious, but the critics felt that Claude had overlooked one main lesson which Nature had tried to teach him in the bay of Matanzas. Especially Dr. E. Bräuer, whose own very thorough calculations had been first announced in 1925, warned Claude that the comparatively warm water that had come up through his too-short cold-water pipe was not the only culprit. It was Dr. Bräuer's contention that it was a mistake to work with low-pressure water vapor. He suggested that Claude should adopt d'Arsonval's proposal for a separate working fluid and use sulfur dioxide, or ammonia. The warm surface water would then play about the same role that the natural steam plays at Larderello. It would merely be the means of heating the working fluid. There would then be no trouble with the salt content of the sea water, and no loss of efficiency due to the air dissolved in the surface water, both factors which had complicated Claude's operations.

Claude did not listen to these well-meant suggestions; he apparently wanted to prove that it would work his way too. The unit on the *Tunisie* differed from the original pilot plant only in size. The ship also carried machinery for utilizing the electric

current used; it was a large refrigerating unit. Claude's imagination was tickled by the paradox of converting the heat of the
tropical seas into ice. The *Tunisie* proceeded to the Atlantic off
Brazil and tests began in 1934. The results were more or less a
repetition of the events in Cuba. The machine finally ran, but
poorly.

In the end Claude was so disgusted that he sank his floating
equipment, picking a spot where the ocean is especially deep.
"An idealist to the last," a German editor commented. "Anybody else would at least have sold it for scrap."

The sad and somewhat flamboyant end of Claude's work does
not prove that it is inherently impossible to extract energy from
the temperature difference between surface and bottom water.
It merely proves that Claude's particular method cannot do it.
If he had followed the suggestions made after the Cuban tests
he might easily have been successful.

D'Arsonval's original article, you remember, stated that the
boiler could be in cold water, provided the condenser is buried
in ice. A compatriot of d'Arsonval's, the physicist Dr. Barjeot,
took up this reasoning some 40 years later. The bottom water
of the oceans, Claude had always pointed out, has a temperature
of 39 degrees Fahrenheit even at the equator. Yes, added Dr.
Barjeot, and in the Arctic too. But the temperature of the air in
the Arctic is *minus* 50 degrees, and often even less, which means
a temperature difference of some 90 degrees Fahrenheit instead
of the 50 degrees which was the best Claude could hope for.
Besides, in the tropics you may *want* energy; in the Arctic you
need it. Another obvious advantage of Barjeot's scheme, as compared to Claude's, is that there is no need for a long pipe. All
that is needed is one long enough to reach through the ice to the

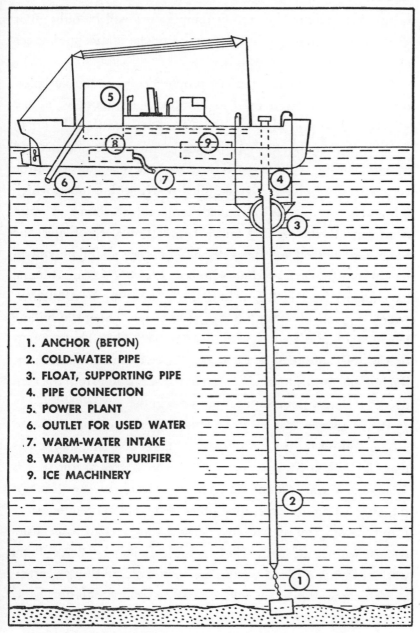

1. ANCHOR (BETON)
2. COLD-WATER PIPE
3. FLOAT, SUPPORTING PIPE
4. PIPE CONNECTION
5. POWER PLANT
6. OUTLET FOR USED WATER
7. WARM-WATER INTAKE
8. WARM-WATER PURIFIER
9. ICE MACHINERY

36. Claude's seaborne power plant, the steamer *Tunisie*

water underneath. The water's temperature will be only 36 or 37 degrees Fahrenheit, but compared to the *minus* 50 degrees above, that is still quite warm.

As working fluid Dr. Barjeot proposed one of the carbohydrates which is often used as "bottled gas," namely butane (C_4H_{10}), which becomes a liquid if the temperature is less than 14 degrees Fahrenheit. Since butane and water do not mix and butane does not even dissolve in water, the machinery can be very simple. You have a boiler, filled partly with butane, which is liquid because of the low outside temperature. Pump up water from beneath the ice and inject it directly into the boiler; the butane will boil off and the water will freeze as a kind of equivalent of the ashes in an ordinary firebox. After the gaseous butane has done its work in the turbine it continues to the condenser, which is partly filled with lumps of salty ice. There the butane becomes a liquid again and if it is not very cold outside, a portion of the salty ice may melt. But the two liquids do not mix, the butane returns to the boiler, and the salt water from the condenser is simply poured out to refreeze in the Arctic cold.

At first glance, the idea of extracting energy from water of a temperature of 37 or 38 degrees Fahrenheit sounds far less reasonable than the idea of getting energy from water that is "nice and warm," around 82 degrees Fahrenheit. But here our thinking is literally determined by our own blood temperature. From the old firebox we have derived the habit of associating energy with heat, with what feels to us like heat. Anything warmer than our blood we declare to be hot; anything appreciably colder we think of as cold. Actually, of course, it is not "heat" that matters, but an available level difference, and this is much higher in the Barjeot scheme than in Claude's. Furthermore the machinery itself is simpler, cheaper, and looks more reliable.

It is too bad that Dr. Barjeot was not a rich man like Claude, so that he might have tried out a pilot plant in northern Canada or in Greenland. Then we would know whether his theory works as planned or whether there are unforeseen difficulties. A test would also show whether the power plant is actually as cheap as Dr. Barjeot himself believes. If it is, it would be cheap enough to be used for only part of the year. Since power needs in settled areas are greatest in winter, such power plants might then be used as winter stand-by plants.

So much for the oceans as a power source by virtue of the temperature differences between surface and bottom. How about the other possibilities?

Ocean waves easily lift steamers weighing 10,000 tons and more for several feet. Obviously these waves contain fantastic energies. Nor does it seem too hard to harness them. An engineer named Josef Wimmer once made what looks like a simple proposal. Put a double row of stout posts into the sea, not too far offshore. The posts, in order to stand any kind of weather for a long time, should be solid concrete-and-steel structures. Arrange a number of floats between these posts, floats of considerable size, comparable to the dimensions of medium-sized freighters. Since the motion of the water in a wave is essentially an up-and-down movement, each incoming wave will lift the heavy floats in neat succession (see fig. 37), with comparatively little scraping of the floats against the posts. All that is then needed is an arrangement of levers attached to the floats to translate their piston-like up-and-down movement into some form of useful power.

So far this sounds all right; in fact, the scheme is oddly familiar, as the term "piston-like" movement indicates. The floats between their posts do what the pistons in an ordinary gasoline engine do; they go up and down. And if that up-and-down movement of the pistons can be translated into useful work, why shouldn't it be possible to do the same with the floats? They are merely much bigger and activated by a different power source. But in these two differences all the difficulties are hidden. In a

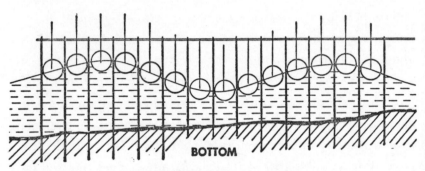

37. Wimmer's wave engine

car engine a 1/4-inch rod will do; with the floats you would need a large steel beam, which weighs more in proportion to its strength. You lose energy because the whole machinery becomes so huge. Where you can rely on a film of oil to reduce friction in the car engine, such a big machine would need complicated arrangements. In the small piston engine you know precisely how much power will be developed in each cylinder, and the strength of all the parts can be calculated accordingly. But for what power do you design the wave engine? If you count on an average, the waves following in the wake of a storm may well tear everything apart. If you design for the maximum which can be expected, everything becomes enormously clumsy and heavy. Somebody once calculated the output to be expected of a set of floats 1200 feet across, with each float 600 feet long. It would probably average 1500 horsepower, less than you can get from a single airplane engine.

Besides, waves are anything but "firm power." To make the wave engine useful a way has to be found to bridge the periods when the sea lies nice and quiet and blue, inviting the engineers and mechanics, overseers and workers, and everybody's families, to take a swim. (The Head Accountant will be missing, however; he'll sit in his office in front of a desk calculator and worry.)

Again it sounds as if it would be very simple to overcome this obstacle. The wave engine need not drive a generator directly. Its action could pump sea water into a large basin, not far from the shoreline but located on a higher level. The water, which would flow steadily, in a well-regulated stream, from the high-level basin back into the sea, would drive water turbines coupled with generators. Such a high-level basin can be built, but not free of charge.

However, there is a way of filling a high-level basin near the shore with sea water and thereby producing firm water power which does not require the cumbersome wave engine. This method is based on a long-known device, the hydraulic ram, first invented in 1796 by Joseph Montgolfier, one of the two brothers who jointly invented the hot-air balloon. The device for "catching" the surf and making it use part of its own energy to lift some of the water to a higher level is based on the simple fact that moving water can push a valve shut. The principle is illustrated in fig. 38. Moving water—a wave—enters a horizontal pipe through the funnel at the left. Since this water is moving

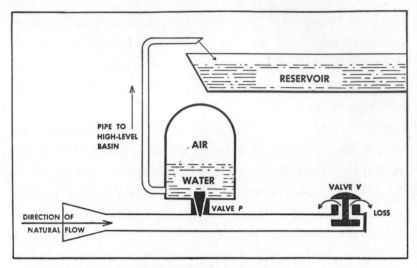

38. Montgolfier's hydraulic ram

Moving water enters a funnel from the left and continues through the pipe to the right until it reaches the valve V. If the water is moving slowly, or not at all, the valve V stays open, since it is quite heavy. The water then simply flows out again around this valve and returns to the sea. But when a wave increases the speed of the water in the pipe, the valve V will be pushed shut, barring the exit. The energy of the moving water has to go somewhere, and it might burst the pipe. But there is another valve at P, which is pushed open. It leads into a large container which is mostly filled with air. Under the shock some of the water forces its way around the valve P into the container. The weight of the water which has forced its way in then closes valve P again, and at about the same moment valve V opens so that the rest of the water can get out. Now the water which entered the large container could do so only by compressing the air in the container. When valve P is shut, the air expands and forces the water into the pipe which leads upward and empties into the high-level basin. Meanwhile the next wave has arrived and pushed valve V shut, and the whole cycle starts over again. Although the action in the horizontal pipe is intermittent, the flow of the water through the vertical pipe is almost uniform, since the trapped air in the container smoothes it out by being compressed and expanding again.

it contains energy which, if there is enough of it, closes a valve, thereby blocking its own exit. But it still has energy which has to be expended somewhere and somehow. The ingenious, though rather simple, construction of Montgolfier's device sees to it that this energy can do only one thing: lift a portion of the water to a higher level.

If this scheme were translated into an actual power plant the high-level basin would have to be quite large because the out-flow from this basin must be steady and may have to bridge periods as long as, say, two weeks, during which the surf may be weak. Naturally some shorelines are more suited for the con-struction of such a power plant than others. The ideal shore would have strong and preferably unceasing surf, a high coast, and a natural depression not far from the sea. If there is a place where this combination exists, some of the surrounding territory probably also drains into the natural depression, thereby assist-ing in producing the all-important steadiness of supply.

I don't know whether such a place exists. If it does, and if the area is also sufficiently settled and industrialized to warrant a power plant, there can be little doubt that hydraulic rams and not pumps operated by a wave engine will be used to fill the high-level basin.

Finally there are the tides.

As distinct from storm waves and surf, the tides have the great advantage that they are not caused by "weather." They are ac-tually an astronomical event, recurring in a regular cycle. Like all astronomical events they can be calculated—meaning pre-dicted—a long time in advance.

The major cause of the tides is the moon; more precisely the moon's gravitational field, which reaches down to the surface of our planet from space, penetrating the earth's gravitational field, which reaches out to the moon. In other words, the moon attracts the earth as the earth attracts the moon. The moon's attraction is naturally best visible when it acts on a substance that offers little resistance to being moved—in this case water, which covers three-quarters of the earth's surface. Out in the open ocean the moon's gravitation causes the water to bulge up slightly; probably the most correct way of saying it is to say that the ocean's surface is deformed by the moon's attraction. If you imagine a line drawn from the moon's center through the center of the earth you'll find that the water around that line is pulled in the direction of the moon by about a yard. The earth as a whole also yields to this attraction and this causes the water on the other side (away from the moon) to be "left behind," making a second bulge which is not quite as high as the bulge on the moonward side.

If the earth turned on its axis at the same rate at which the moon goes around the earth, these two bulges would remain in the same place and might go unnoticed. But the earth turns, and both bulges seem to wander around the globe. I say "seem to wander," because they do not actually travel. It is merely that the moon always deforms the water directly below it and directly away from it. Whatever happens to lie along and in the continuation of the center-to-center line is raised by a yard. The center of the bulge is not precisely on that line; the deforming of the ocean takes a little time, and the center of the bulge lags behind the apparent motion of the moon.

In addition, the sun also produces two bulges, one in the direction of the sun, the other away from it. The solar bulges are much smaller than the lunar bulges, even though the sun is much bigger than the moon, because the sun is much farther away. It is only 240,000 miles to the moon but 93 million miles to the sun.

At new moon and at full moon the solar and lunar bulges lie in the same direction and the tides are especially high. If the moon forms its bulge where the sun produces a low spot the tide will appear to be rather low.

In the open ocean all this is quite gentle. The dramatic effects take place at the shore, especially if the shoreline is indented so that it serves as a funnel for the tidal bulge. In such a case the average bulge height of 1 yard literally piles up into something impressive. At the mouth of the Severn River in England a 25-foot tide is the rule and the tide can be as high as 47 feet. In the Bay of Fundy, Nova Scotia, even the weakest tide raises the water level by 21 feet, while a good high tide, when the sun is collaborating with the moon, will mount to more than 52 feet.

To a very minor extent tidal streams have been utilized in Europe for the last thousand years. There is documentary evidence for a tidal mill in northwest Germany around 980 A.D. We don't know how that looked, but the tidal mills which were built (and described) later were the same as the water mills built farther inland. Nor was the practice restricted to the European mainland; the English built tidal mills too. The first water-pumping system of the City of London was operated by means of a paddlewheel installed in London Bridge. European immigrants carried the practice to the New World, and large numbers of small tidal mills were built along the New England coast in the course of the centuries. One of them, furnishing power for a sawmill, is said to be still operating in Maine.

Modern engineering projects dealing with tidal power began to be published in large numbers soon after the First World War. It happens that in respect to tidal power the United States comes off a very poor second or third in comparison to other countries. There is no suitable place on the Atlantic Coast south of Maine and none at all along the Pacific Coast except in Alaska.

But there are many good places in France, both along the coast of the Bay of Biscay in the west and along the Channel coast. Leafing through bound volumes of French engineering journals one gets the impression that a large percentage of the French engineers living along these coasts devoted their evenings and weekends to studying detailed charts of the various river mouths and sketching tentative plans for power dams to catch the tides. In the late 1920s the French even got a pilot plant going. It was located in the Département Finistère, the extreme western end of France, formerly known as the province of Brittany. There a small river, the Diouris, empties into the English Channel, due north of the well-known port of Brest. The river has been dammed, but the river water was used only when the tidal current was at a standstill. The normal time interval between one high tide and the next is 12 hours and 25 minutes; the tidal power plant, with some 2500-horsepower output, operated for about 10 hours out of each such cycle. The river power plant then filled in for the remaining 2½ hours. Most of the current was used in Brest in the government arsenal.

There are various ways in which a tidal power plant can be run. The simplest has been named the "one-basin scheme." Supposing you have a good tide, say 20 feet or better, in an estuary with a channel narrow enough to build a dam across. The dam will be provided with gates, and as the tide "comes in" all gates

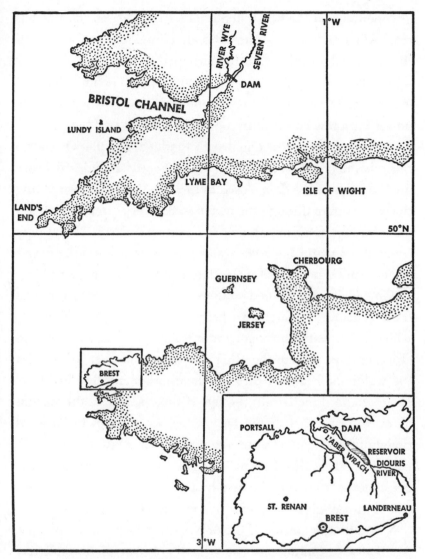

39. Site of the experimental tidal power plant in Brittany, showing also the location of the Severn River Project in England

are open so that the tide will fill the estuary. When the tide has reached its highest level the gates are closed and you wait until the level outside the gate has dropped a useful amount, say 5 feet. Then the water trapped in the estuary behind the dam is permitted to escape—through the turbines. This will provide power for a few hours, until the water level behind the dam has decreased to be almost equal with the level outside. Of course this scheme could be operated "the other way round," by keeping the gates of the dam closed as the tide rises and then letting the water run in through the turbines. But very often the estuary will also be a river mouth and the dam will hold back not only trapped sea water but river water too. In such cases the power period can be prolonged if the dam is operated "outgoing."

Somewhat more refined, and also more expensive, is the two-basin scheme, in which two basins are separated by the dam which contains the turbogenerator units. One basin is operated at a higher level than the other and the turbines can discharge the water that has run through them either into the low-level basin or else directly into the sea. If the opening of the various gates, from the sea to the basins, and from basin to basin, is timed properly, you can run the power plant without any slack periods, getting the "firm power" so strongly demanded by the consumers. However, the two-basin scheme will produce less power at any given moment than the one-basin scheme.

Naturally the output of the one-basin power plant will vary. At about two times a day you get no power at all. Twice a day also (the periods slowly shift around the clock since two tidal cycles take very nearly 25 hours) you get peak power, probably more than is needed. This fact makes another two-basin scheme possible. Here you have a second high-level basin into which

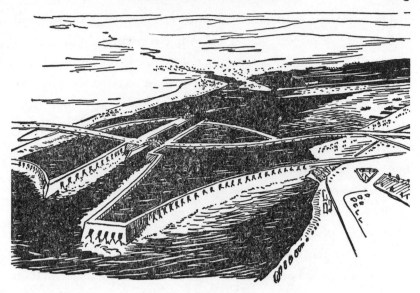

40. The British Severn River Project

water is pumped with the surplus power of the peak production period. This water can then be used to bridge the slack period. This is actually a method of storing energy and, except in a dry and hot climate where the evaporation losses would be high, is a reasonably efficient one.

There are a few places on earth where conditions for tidal power plants are known to be most favorable, and a tidal power plan exists for each place. These are the Severn River Project in England, the Rance River Project in France, the Petitcodiac (Bay of Fundy) Project in Canada, the Passamaquoddy Project in the United States, and the Bahía Nueva Project in Argentina. More or less extensive studies have been made about every one of them, and the Passamaquoddy Project was even actually started at one time. But the one most likely to become reality first is the Severn River Project.

The reason no large-scale tidal power plant has yet been built is that such a project would be rather expensive both in construction and upkeep and could not compete with other types of power plants. But as the fossil fuels diminish, the gap between the price of a kilowatt from fuel and that of one from tidal power will shrink. Most likely England will be the country in which tidal power will become economically feasible first, because other power will become more expensive first.

The Severn River flows into the Bristol Channel, and because of the funneling action of this channel the mouth of the Severn has the exceptionally high tides that have been described. If the Severn were dammed at about the point where the river Wye joins it, one would get a rather large one-basin scheme. The dam would have to be about 2½ miles long. The proponents of the plan have pointed out that, since a bridge across the river at or near this point has been planned for a long time, the crown of the power dam could serve as a bridge. The project would be quite expensive; in 1930 it was estimated at 150 million dollars, which critics declared was rather optimistic. In all probability it would cost three times as much, but it would also produce 2000 million kilowatt-hours of electricity per year, which amounts to a yearly saving of nearly a million tons of coal.

The Bay of Fundy, which almost separates Nova Scotia from the Canadian mainland, has two tidal power projects. One is a Canadian project usually labeled with the name of the Petit-codiac River. The river widens into Shepody Bay, which is in turn an arm of Chignecto Bay, which is an arm of the Bay of Fundy. An important consideration is that there is, next to the Petitcodiac estuary, another one, the Memramcook estuary, separated from the first by a narrow rock ridge, almost like a

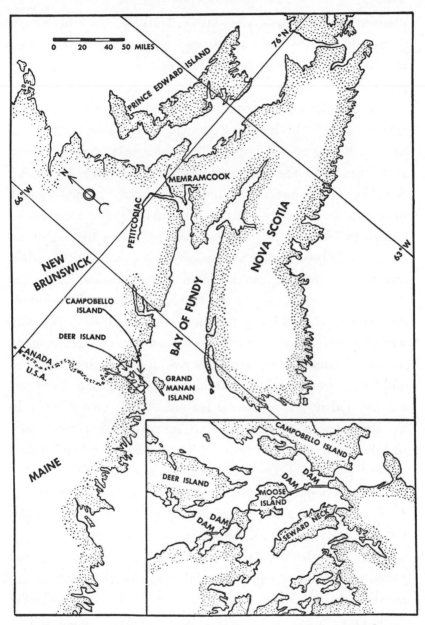

41. The Bay of Fundy, with possible sites for tidal power plants

planned dam for a two-basin scheme. The project would be comparatively easy to build and would have a power production roughly half that of the Severn Project. But at the present moment it would not pay.

This was also said about the second tidal power project in the Bay of Fundy, the Passamaquoddy Project. Passamaquoddy Bay is at—or forms—the border between Maine and New Brunswick. There are a number of islands in the bay which could be used as anchors for the power dams. The first project, developed in the early 1920s by Dexter P. Cooper, proposed a two-basin scheme, with Passamaquoddy Bay as the high-level pool and Cobscook Bay as the low-level pool. The Canadian government at first approved the plan generally but later withdrew its approval because it was feared that the use of the whole area might be harmful to the local fishing industry. The plan was then modified to use only American waters and American islands. Fortunately the coastline is so indented and irregular, and the distribution of the natural islands is such, that engineers are not tied down by natural features to just one scheme. In the Passamaquoddy area there are so many different possibilities that even with the restriction to American land and waters either type of tidal power plant could be created. It could be a one-basin scheme with a rather high output but two dead periods per day, or a two-basin scheme with a far lower output but firm power around the clock.

In 1935 the United States government became actively engaged in the Passamaquoddy tidal power project. Preliminary construction was begun under the Federal Emergency Relief Appropriation Act, but one year later Congress balked and no additional money was appropriated, so the project had to be shelved. Chief spokesman against the Passamaquoddy project was the late Senator Arthur H. Vandenberg, who engaged in a violent campaign against what he called a $36,000,000 boondoggle. He stated that a coal-burning power plant with the same output of kilowatt hours could be built for $16,000,000. Probably correct, but the coal would have to be transported there first. And apparently it never occurred to either Senator Vandenberg or any of his numerous supporters that a century from now there would be little coal but the tides would still be active. In February 1954 the Senate reconsidered and passed (without debate or dissent) a bill appropriating $3,000,000 for a new survey. Passamaquoddy may still become the first large tidal power plant.

Similar cost calculations probably led to the abandonment, or at least the indefinite postponement, of the Argentine tidal power project. It had been carefully worked out by Argentine government experts and was discussed at length by engineers from many countries on the occasion of the Second World Power Conference in Berlin in 1930. In southern Argentina just south of the Gulf of San Matías is the Váldez Peninsula. On the map it looks very much like a mushroom growing out of the mainland and on either side it is flanked by a bay. The bay to the south has the name of Bahía Nueva; the one to the north is called the Gulf of San José. A tidal power plant would work in either of these bays, for the tides can be as high as 50 feet, but the government experts decided in favor of the Gulf of San José because a far shorter dam, only 4½ miles in length, would be needed to close it. The bay is generally shallow, around 100 feet deep, but covers an area of very nearly 300 square miles. The fact that there are two bays in close proximity was also advantageous, not to provide for a two-basin scheme—the peninsula

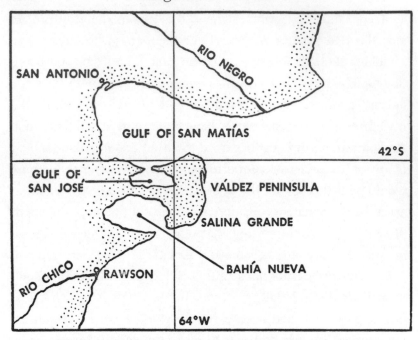

42. The Gulf of San José and Bahía Nueva in Argentina

is too wide for that—but because the dam could be uninterrupted. There would be no need to provide for the passage of ships, since the shipping could as easily go into Bahía Nueva.

The concrete dam was to be so high that its crown would be 6 feet above the highest flood level ever recorded. The turbines built into the dam were designed to operate on a level difference as small as 20 inches so that the periods of enforced rest would be only 75 minutes each. Total power output was calculated to be 5500 million kilowatt-hours per year, about equivalent to 2,250,000 tons of coal per year. Argentina has to import its fossil fuel, having very little of its own, but at present even imported coal can still compete with tidal power.

9. HARNESSING THE WINDS

43. Honnef wind tower, designed in 1928, but never built

Harnessing the Winds

Just how unreliable is the wind?

Well, that literally depends on where you look. In New York and New Jersey it may be a fine example of something not to be trusted. In Antarctica, on the other hand, one spot had a steady gale of more than 45 miles per hour for 7 months without any interruption.

With all the natural distrust one may feel about the reliability of the wind one must admit that wind power has been of great importance in history. It was the first natural power used by mankind. For many centuries ships moved by wind power or they did not move, unless they were small enough to rely on muscle power in a calm sea. Mankind discovered and explored the distant places on this planet mostly by wind power—that is, when exploring journeys could be made by ship. The occasional attempts to power land vehicles by means of sails failed; the "wind wagon" of an enterprising Dutchman, which excited his contemporaries almost three centuries ago, was a sporting device rather than a means of transportation. The same is true of its off-spring, the iceboat, although there have been many more of those.

But while the wind could not be harnessed by our forefathers for land transportation, for many centuries it did something even more important: it ground the grain for the daily bread. A fact not known to the many generations of windmillers in the Christian kingdoms of the European North during the late Middle Ages and early modern times is that they were using a "heathen device," for the windmill seems to have been invented by the Arabs. It appeared in northern Europe in the twelfth century, after the early Crusades, and first became common in Germany and the Netherlands. For the Dutch, wind power was the means of literally making their country—their windmills pumped their made land dry. Elsewhere wind power pumped water too, but for the opposite reason—to irrigate the crops. Even now in the United States and Canada about half a million pumping windmills are doing their chore almost daily.

Navigation by wind power was not a matter of choice until steam was harnessed. But the other uses all tend to demonstrate the unreliability of the wind. All these are chores which have to be done, but not at regular intervals or according to a strict timetable. You can grind enough grain to last for months with a few days' work in a windmill and it does not matter much just when you start. Irrigation is virtually a hallmark of unfirm power, as we know from the discussion of solar energy. Mention of solar energy at this point is not purely accidental; wind—not its direction, which is influenced by the earth's rotation and many other factors—is the direct result of solar energy.

Now if wind is a form of solar energy and its main drawback is its unreliability, couldn't we solve the problem by using solar energy to make a reliable wind?

This question is sheer nonsense if you have in mind a wind

from east to west or from south to north. But, under certain conditions and with certain restrictions, it might be possible to make a vertical wind.

The idea was developed by the French physicist Bernard Dubos and submitted to the French Academy of Sciences at about the time Georges Claude submitted his plans. Amusingly the two plans even show a few similarities because both are based on differences in temperature levels. The Academy— usually considered conservative by its friends and reactionary by its enemies—recommended that Dubos's idea be followed up, especially in French North Africa, which has no fuel and needs power. As a matter of fact Dubos had the North African Atlas mountains in mind when he developed his plans.

To make a powerful vertical wind, he said, you need a hot desert plain under a mostly cloudless sky and, in the near neighborhood, fairly high mountains with nearly vertical faces. In the desert plain the air pressure will probably be near normal, balancing a column of 760 millimeters of mercury. On the mountain top, an assumed 6600 feet above the desert, the pressure will be around 595 millimeters of mercury. In addition to that, and more important, the temperature of the air on top of the mountain will be somewhere between 30 and 40 degrees Fahrenheit, while the air just over the desert sands will be between 100 and 110 degrees. Normally the air between the desert and the mountain top will be quietly layered with slowly decreasing temperatures and pressures as you go up. But if you opened an avenue for the hot desert air, using the equivalent of an enormous chimney, a storm unparalleled in speed in Nature would develop inside the chimney, neatly packaged in the pipe

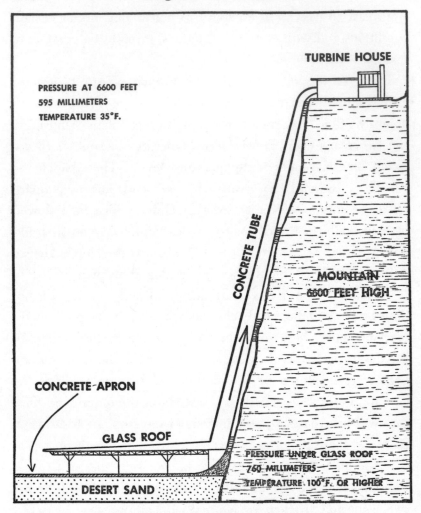

PRESSURE AT 6600 FEET
595 MILLIMETERS
TEMPERATURE 35°F.

TURBINE HOUSE

CONCRETE TUBE

MOUNTAIN
6600 FEET HIGH

CONCRETE-APRON

GLASS ROOF

PRESSURE UNDER GLASS ROOF
760 MILLIMETERS
TEMPERATURE 100°F. OR HIGHER

DESERT SAND

44. Principle of Professor Dubos's power plant

and ready for exploitation. One could count on a speed of about 180 feet per second; the volume of air moving at this speed would depend mostly on the chimney's diameter.

The wind turbine that utilized this typhoon in a pipe would have to be at the upper end, on top of the mountain. The moun-

tain would also support the chimney, which would be anchored
to its side. In order to make the scheme effective, the supply of
heated air must be steady, and no heat must be lost through the
walls of the chimney. The supply could be improved by having
the chimney flare out at the bottom into a large glass-roofed
area. The necessary insulation of the chimney could be ac-
complished most simply if the enormous pipe—it should have a
diameter of about 30 feet—were made of porous cement, which
is not very heavy and is a fine insulator.

When finished, a power plant designed along these lines
would look rather like some water-power plants which have
enormous penstocks coming down a mountainside. But in these
plants the movement through the penstocks is down; in a Dubos
power plant it would be up. There is little doubt that a Dubos
power plant would work. Whether it would work efficiently is
another question which probably cannot be answered without
first building and studying a pilot plant.

Another French idea for the utilization of wind power, developed by the researchers of the aerodynamical institute at
St. Cyr, somewhat resembles Dubos's scheme in that it also
works with a "chimney." But the dimensions are much smaller
and the principle is entirely different. The device consists of a
sheet-metal chimney just strong enough to stand up under wind,
which is open on top and has a number of large holes around
the bottom so that the air can enter freely. The height of such a
chimney would be about 60 to 75 feet. At its crown a "collar"
is attached, a fairly short section of a similar chimney of double
the diameter. This collar is held in place by narrow supporting
struts, so that air can enter into the space between chimney and
collar without any obstruction. If such a device is exposed to

wind, no matter from which direction, the wind, blowing through the space between collar and chimney, will cause a movement of air through the chimney itself. In the chimney the air can go only one way—it can enter through the holes near the bottom and escape from the open top. The turbine is located in the chimney above the air holes.

There can be no doubt that this device is as simple and as cheap as one could wish, but apparently it is still too expensive to compete with coal under the conditions prevailing in France at the present time.

To go back to the starting point of our discussion: wind is as unreliable as it is cheap. Yes, but . . . and this "but" means several things. It means "but we would like to use it anyhow." It also means "but we'll soon have to grab any power source we can." And finally it means "but wind is unreliable only near the ground; higher up it becomes a fairly dependable proposition."

On the premise that the wind is far more reliable 1000 to 1500 feet above the ground, a German engineer, Hermann Honnef, has been campaigning since about 1925 for 1000-foot wind towers with enormous windmill wheels. He claimed that such generators would work for as much as 4000 hours per year. Since a year has 8766 hours this would still be less than half the time, and Honnef's critics have stated that his figures were too large in any case. For many years Honnef suffered one setback after another. He was turned down by three successive German governments and then by the Marshall Plan administrators. But in 1953 the citizens of the small south German town of Salach, not far from Stuttgart, raised the money for a much smaller Honnef tower which is to have a wind-catching impeller 130 feet in diameter. Salach normally produces the electric current it needs

in an ordinary coal-burning power plant. If the Honnef generator works nicely it will save coal. If it hits a slack period the old
power plant can be fired up to serve as the stand-by power so
necessary to all installations depending upon an essentially unreliable source.

What encouraged the people of Salach to take this step is an
American example. A really large wind generator worked faith-
fully for years, on a mountain called Grandpa's Knob, near Rutland, Vermont. There is often a steady breeze on top of a ridge
of hills even though down in the valley the air seems perfectly
quiet. In 1939 a Boston engineer, Palmer Cosslet Putnam, had
the idea that a hilltop should be a suitable place for a wind
generator. Since aviation engineers had gained considerable
knowledge of how air flows around an airplane wing, a wind
generator could be designed far more efficiently in 1939 than it
could have been only two decades earlier.[1]

The tower for the wind turbine on Grandpa's Knob was only
125 feet tall, just tall enough to carry the two-bladed impeller,
which had a diameter of 175 feet. Each blade looked very much
like an airplane wing and the whole was mounted in such a way
that it turned into the wind automatically. The turbine was
ready for operation on October 19, 1941, and ran virtually without serious interruption until March 1945. Then the wind

---

[1] In windmill design, engineers always ask about the ratio of blade-tip speed
to wind velocity. This ratio is almost always larger than 1, which means that the
tips of the blades will travel at a higher speed than 30 miles per hour in a 30-
mile-per-hour wind. In a very slow, multibladed windmill this ratio is about 1.5
to 1 so that, again in a 30-mile-per-hour wind, the tips of the blades will travel
at the rate of 45 miles per hour. In the "classical" windmill of Dutch paintings,
the ratio is about 2 to 1, or slightly faster; in more modern windmills it is around
3 to 1. The wind generator on Grandpa's Knob had a blade-tip velocity of 180
miles per hour, so that the ratio was around 6 to 1. For the most modern designs
with narrow propeller-like blades the ratio will be still higher.

generator on Grandpa's Knob became a war casualty. On the twenty-sixth of March one of the two blades was torn loose. Since the generator was spinning at the moment, the loose blade smashed into the other one, damaging it badly. If that had happened in normal times the damaged blades would have been carefully inspected, and the accident would have resulted in newer and better blades. But it happened during the Second World War. Neither material nor labor could be obtained, and since the wind generator could not be classed as "vital"—after all it was mostly experimental, even though it did produce current which it fed into the local network—the structure had to be abandoned.

In spite of this ultimate failure this generator had been the most important step forward in the development of wind power. Its operation had furnished engineers with information and data on the design of large wind-power units, or "aerogenerators," as they are also called. The most complete study of the possibilities of aerogenerators as a source of commercial power has been made in this country by Percy H. Thomas, a Senior Engineer (now retired) of the Federal Power Commission. The study showed that wind actually is far more reliable about 500 feet above ground than at ground level. It also showed that the monthly average which could be expected for a given place was surprisingly stable. There was an enormous amount of research material available for this study because the United States Weather Bureau maintains hundreds of weather stations at which wind velocity and direction are measured every hour as part of the routine. A tabulation of all these records showed that there is generally less wind from June through September and more wind from October through May. But if, say, Kansas City

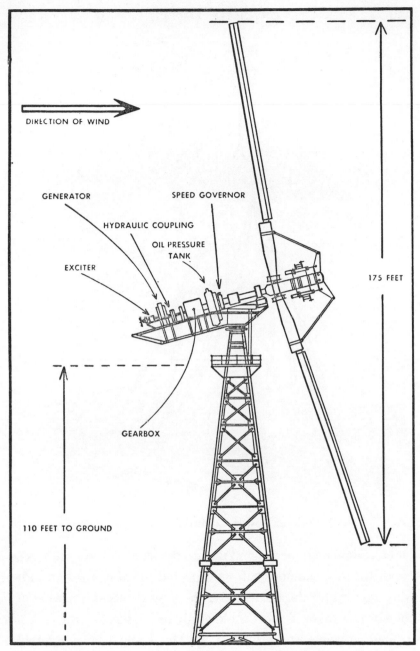

DIRECTION OF WIND

GENERATOR

SPEED GOVERNOR

HYDRAULIC COUPLING

OIL PRESSURE
TANK

EXCITER

175 FEET

GEARBOX

110 FEET TO GROUND

45. The wind turbine on Grandpa's Knob, near Rutland, Vermont

46. A Federal Power Commission aerogenerator

had a certain amount of wind during the month of May in 1953, about the same amount can be expected for May 1954 and for May 1955. Since the records also show what places are windier than others, favored spots could easily be chosen.

The aerogenerator proposed by Mr. Thomas is a 235-foot bridge, carrying a wind turbine at each end. The center of this bridge is mounted on a turntable on a 475-foot tower so that the whole bridge can be turned around. Of course one such generator would do little good. Long chains of them must be built, with electrical interconnections so that if two or three generators out of a chain of a dozen happen to be becalmed, the others can do the work. But even with chains of aerogenerators covering areas of hundreds of square miles it would still be risky to rely on wind power exclusively. Mr. Thomas therefore suggested integrating the wind power plants with hydroelectric power plants, letting the wind do the work as and when it pleases, with reservoirs of river water as stand-bys for calm periods or times of exceptional power demand.

Since aerogenerators are cheaper by far than tidal power plants they may come soon, but only where water power has been developed already.

10. NEW LAND

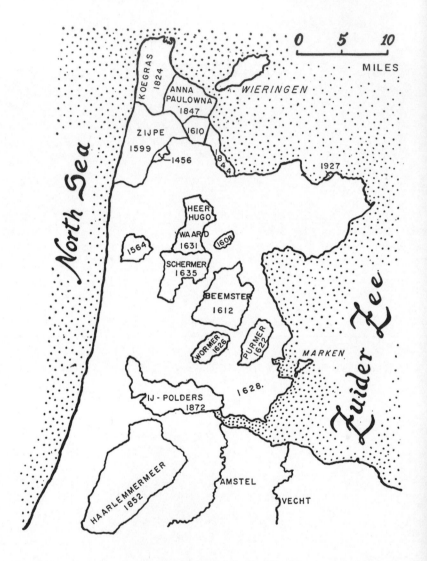

47. The provinces of North and South Holland, showing land reclamation of the past

New Land

Try to picture a scene which must have taken place many a time in the European universities about the year 1400 A.D. Half a dozen scholars and one or two Dominican friars are standing around a large oaken table engaged in a discussion for the benefit of the Duke and the Bishop, who are seated at the table. A parchment map of the world is spread on the table; it is supposed to have been copied from a copy of a copy of a map originally drawn under the supervision of the great Ptolemy in the second century A.D.

The debate deals with the question of whether or not there is a large continent in the Southern Hemisphere. It is a difficult problem because the sources disagree—remember that neither the scholars, nor the friars, nor the Bishop, nor even the Duke has ever traveled beyond a radius of more than, say, 200 miles.

On Ptolemy's map, the east coast of Africa suddenly turns eastward, about ten degrees south of the equator, forming a southern shore for the Indian Ocean and uniting with southern Asia in the vicinity of Java. As Ptolemy's map includes only part of the Southern Hemisphere, one cannot tell how far this land extends to the south, but evidently it is a very large land mass.

On the other hand, the Greek historian Herodotus had re-

235

ported that a party of Phoenicians, financed by the Egyptian Pharaoh Necho, had sailed around Africa, starting from the east coast of Egypt and returning through the Strait of Gibraltar. If that was true, the large land mass pictured by Ptolemy did not exist. Herodotus himself had doubted the Phoenicians' story, because the sailors had reported that when they rounded the southern tip of Africa, the sun had been to the north. But the scholars of 1400 A.D. can explain this: to Herodotus the earth had been flat; since about the time of Ptolemy, however, every educated man had known that it was a sphere and would expect somebody far south of the equator to see the sun to the north.

Since Ptolemy said one thing and Herodotus another, the scholars and churchmen have to try to find the answer by logical reasoning. The scholars point out that there seem to be more stars in the Northern Hemisphere. Whether the stars had pulled the land to the north, or whether the land had pulled the stars to the north was hard to decide, but the indication is that there is less land in the south. The friars mention that the Lord has given the earth to Man to dwell upon, and, since Man cannot dwell on the oceans, it is self-evident that there has to be more land on earth than water. Hence, an enormous continent, at least similar to that drawn by Ptolemy, has to exist.

The Bishop approves this reasoning. But the Duke is inclined to agree with the scholars, and the discussion ends on a note of despair. This is an insoluble problem, and both the scholars and the churchmen are in full agreement that insoluble problems should not exist.

We now know, of course, that there is far more water area on our planet than land area. Even with the addition of the

American double-continent, still unknown in scholastic circles in 1400, though some seafaring men had an inkling of its existence, the ratio is three to one; about 75 per cent of the planet's surface is covered by water and only about 25 per cent is land.

Since no new land can be discovered, thinking has been directed toward making the existing land habitable, if it is not. Literally making new land is rarely possible. There are off-shore areas in various places—for example, the west coast of Korea—where the sea is so shallow that one might think of reclaiming some land. But such land reclamation would be fantastically expensive and extremely difficult.

It so happens, however, that there is one region where land reclamation not only is possible but can be made to pay, as well. Coincidentally, this area also has been inhabited since prehistoric times. It is the European shore along the North Sea, from the mouth of the Elbe River westward to the area of Dunkerque. Because this area has "always" been inhabited, land reclamation is a tradition; in fact, the map we now view would look entirely different if the land there had been "untouched by human hands." The people who excelled in this land-making, and who will continue to excel, are the Dutch. Any almanac will tell you that the area of the Kingdom of the Netherlands, to use its official name, is about 12,500 square miles. But if the Dutch had not built their dikes, about 6800 of these square miles would be covered by water at high tide and would be uninhabitable, if only because the salty water of the North Sea would ruin all edible crops.

Much of the Netherlands actually *is* reclaimed land, especially in the two provinces of North Holland and South Holland. North Holland is the region north of the old university town of Leiden

with the city of Amsterdam at its approximate center. The next
largest Dutch city, Rotterdam, is the approximate center of
South Holland. The battle of these two provinces against the
North Sea is virtually over. Right now the main activity is in
the province south of South Holland; namely, the province of
Zeeland which consists almost exclusively of low islands.

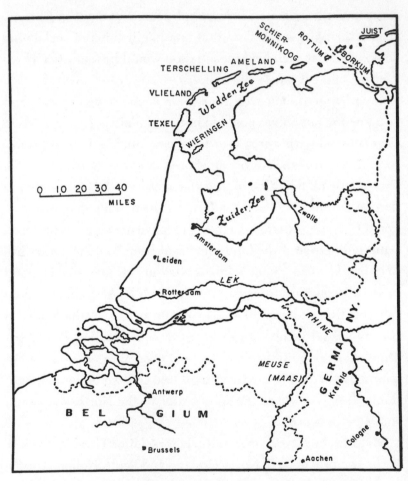

48. Sketch map of the Kingdom of the Netherlands in 1900

The watery geography of the provinces of Holland and Zeeland is determined by three rivers, all of which have their
sources outside the country. The northernmost of the three is
the Rhine which, as it enters Dutch territory, forms two
branches. One is called the Waal. This branch then joins the
Meuse to make the Upper Merwede. The other arm of the
Rhine is called first the Lower Rhine and then the Lek, but
the portion of the Lek near its mouth is called the New Meuse,
presumably due to an old misunderstanding, for the Meuse (or
Maas) is the river to the south of the Rhine which widens into
the Hollandsch Diep before it empties into the North Sea. The
third river is the Schelde, which begins to widen just as soon
as it has passed Antwerp.

At one time all this territory was under Roman occupation,
and it would be most interesting if some Roman had drawn a
map for us of the country as it looked when he was commander
of a legion. Actually Roman writers wrote very little about the
country, most likely because it was not worth anything to them
in its natural state. Only three classical sources are known to me:
Cornelius Tacitus (in his *Germania*), Pomponius Mela (in his
De Chorographia), and, of course, Gaius Plinius Secundus,
Pliny the Elder (in his *Natural History*). Pomponius Mela wrote
just one sentence about the current Holland. "Then it [the
Rhine] is no longer a river but an enormous lake covering a large
area, called Flevo." (. . . "*sed ingens lacus, ubi campos im-
plevit, Flevo dicitur*," in the original wording.) Tacitus men-
tioned the Frisians, whom he divided into "Great" and "Little"
Frisians, saying that they lived along the Rhine up to the North
Sea, and that "both nations also live by the immense lake on
which Roman ships sailed." The most accurate writer, as usual,

was Pliny, who stated that the Rhine, in that area, had three arms named Helium (the westernmost), Rhenus (the center arm), and Flevum (the arm that goes to the north). "In the north the Rhine widens into the lake, in the west it empties into the Meuse." One of Pliny's commentators added that in 12 B.C. the Roman general Drusus Germanicus (also known as Drusus Senior) connected Flevo Lake with the Rhine, probably following the bed of the river Yssel (in Dutch *IJssel*).

All this is not too helpful now, but a few facts emerge. River water made a very large lake, probably in the southern part of what later became the Zuider Zee, while at least one arm of the Rhine seems to have merged inland with the Meuse. The complete picture is that of an area where a canoe was far more useful than a horse and which, consequently, did not interest the Romans, who liked firm ground and were partial to paved highways.

Since two Dutch words will crop up frequently in what follows, they should be explained in advance. The word *Zee* (pronounced "zay") refers to a body of salt water, while the word *Meer* (pronounced "mare") means a body of fresh water. This is somewhat confusing, because two German words which have almost the same spelling and exactly the same pronunciation happen to have opposite meanings, or very nearly so. A German *See* (pronounced "zay") is a fresh-water lake if used with the masculine article, and a body of salt water if used with the feminine article. And the German word *Meer* (pronounced "mare") means the ocean. One sometimes feels that a good alternate word for "language" would be "chaos."

In any event, the Dutch wrested land from both the salty Zee and the fresh-water Meer by building dikes, filling in, and draining. But in spite of hard work through many generations, the over-all balance did not look good. A Dutch government pamphlet states that between 1200 and about 1900 A.D. the Dutch reclaimed land to the following extent:

> 940,000 acres along the seashore
> 345,000 acres by draining lakes
> ———————
> 1,285,000 acres total

But during the same period they lost 1,400,000 acres!

The name of that loss was the Zuider Zee.

The formation of the Zuider Zee is easy to explain. The whole region was below sea level with its deepest portion filled by Flevo Lake. But a great deal of the Zuider Zee area was land, because higher land near the shore protected it from the North Sea. The catastrophe which flooded the low-lying basin with salt water came as a stormy spring tide on All Saints' Day of 1170 A.D. On that day the North Sea tore two pieces of land from the North Holland province, creating the two islands of Wieringen and Texel. About a century later, on Christmas Day, 1277, the North Sea finally broke through, flooding the whole area and producing the Zuider Zee.

In 1277 nobody thought of doing anything about this. But a few centuries later, presumably encouraged by successful dike-building on a smaller scale, some Dutchmen began to wonder whether or not the work of the North Sea might be undone. A study by Hendrick Stevin, published in 1667 under the title "How the Fury of the North Sea May Be Stopped and Holland May Be Protected against It" was the first printed report to consider draining the Zuider Zee. During the following 150 years the idea of reclaiming the area covered by the Zuider Zee was expounded quite often in the Netherlands (some Germans also gave good advice from across the border), but it became a theme like that of the railway tunnel from Calais to Dover: much literature and no action.

The reason there was no action was very simple: any Zuider Zee plan would require a colossal investment. If the plan succeeded, this investment would be recovered, and, in time, large profits would be made. But if it failed, for any one of a dozen different reasons, the investment would be a total loss.

In the meantime another project simply had to be tackled. There were two bodies of fresh water which offered a threat to Amsterdam, the capital. One of them was the *IJ* (the Dutch treat "ij" as *one* letter; hence, the double capital in words such as IJssel. This is pronounced simply as long *i*), which had an open connection to the Zuider Zee; the other was the *Haarlem-mermeer*. The Dutch government earmarked the sum of 8,355,-000 guilders in 1837 to get rid of the menace. Work began three years later and lasted a dozen years. The government somewhat ruefully stated that it had cost 13,789,377 guilders (roughly equivalent to seven and a half million dollars in 1852). But the project had been a success, even though another 20 years of work were needed to change the newly won acres into fruitful land.

The Dutch call a section of reclaimed land a "polder"; the term used for reclaiming land can therefore be Anglicized as "impoldering." When the IJ polder and the Haarlemmermeer polder were still wet, three scientists and engineers—van Diggelen, Kloppenburg, and Faddegon—published a similar scheme for the Zuider Zee. An enormous dike was to close the mouth of the big bay; the trapped water was to be pumped out slowly; and the two rivers, the IJssel and Amstel, which empty into the Zuider Zee, were to be diverted directly into the North Sea. The estimated cost was 92 million guilders.

As more and more projects were published or submitted officially, in the form of memoranda, the government felt that there should be a body of experts which could judge the feasibility of the various plans. Thus an evaluation group, the *Zuiderzeevereeniging*, was established which, directly and indirectly, produced several drafts of bills for the reclamation of the Zuider Zee. But the proposals remained drafts, as the danger of spending scores of millions of guilders without guarantee of success was still too great.

To see what type of land would result from impoldering the Zuider Zee, extensive drilling was carried out (one source says 2188 test drillings were made), and it became clear that about three-fourths of the Zuider Zee area could be made into valuable land. Three men especially were the driving spirits: Van Diggelen, Dr. Cornelis Lely, and the head of the evaluation group, Dr. A. Buma. A complete plan was finished in 1892. But this took time; the turning point was probably the speech made by Queen Wilhelmina of the Netherlands on the occasion of the opening of Parliament in September 1913. The speech contained the following sentences: "I consider the time has come to undertake the enclosure and reclamation of the Zuider Zee. The result will be improved water-control conditions in the adjacent provinces, extension of territory, and a permanent increase in the opportunities of employment."

If times had been normal, the Queen's words probably would have caused quick action. But times were not normal; the First

World War was brewing, and, though the Netherlands intended to stay neutral, it was by no means impossible that the people might have had to defend themselves. In any event, it was not a project to be started while a major war was going on. The decision to attack the Zuider Zee was made in an Act of Parliament passed on June 14, 1918. The scheme to be followed was that of Dr. Cornelis Lely.

It differed from other and earlier schemes in preserving a body of water in the Zuider Zee area. The older schemes had proposed closing up the whole bay and rerouting the rivers so that they would empty into the North Sea, rather than into the Zuider Zee. Dr. Lely pointed out that this might lead to floods farther inland if, as can happen, a storm-driven flood raised for a few days the level of the coastal waters of the North Sea above the level of the rivers. Moreover, Dr. Lely did not want to kill the Zuider Zee fisheries. Finally, he wanted the newly won land to be accessible by water. In short, Dr. Lely suggested creating a number of very large islands within the basin instead of drying up the whole bottom of the bay.

The over-all scheme, then, envisaged first the construction of the main dike, from the island of Wieringen to Friesland at the eastern shore of the Zuider Zee. Then, two large polders were to be started; one, going south from the island of Wieringen, was to be 49,000 acres in extent. This was first called the Northwest Polder, but later the name was changed to Wieringermeer Polder. The other polder was to be south of Friesland, the Northeast Polder, 119,000 acres in extent; it is, incidentally, the only one which has retained its original, and purely geographical, name. Then the Southeast Polder, the biggest of them all, 235,000 acres, was to be tackled. Since that time its name has been changed to Flevoland as this is the probable area of *Flevo lacus* of the Romans. Also, the project for this polder has been subdivided into two phases, East Flevoland and South Flevoland, which when finished are to be only one polder. The last of the projected polders was the Southwest Polder, 150,000 acres, now called Markerwaard.

The remaining body of water would then have an area of nearly 250,000 acres. It had to be large enough to receive the waters of the IJssel and other smaller rivers, even when the level of the salt water outside the main dike would be higher than that of the water inside the dike, so no water could be discharged into the North Sea. And under bad flood conditions this peculiar circumstance might go on for some time; there had to be a basin to hold the river water until it could be discharged. In the course of time this basin would become fresh water; hence, it should no longer be called by its old name. No longer Zuider Zee but IJsselmeer.

Work started in 1927, and three things were tackled simultaneously—the main dike, the Wieringermeer Polder, and a 100-acre trial polder which was named Andijk. The trial polder was used for experiments to find out how the land should be treated after it had been impoldered. Obviously, farmers could not go ahead and try to sow wheat or to plant beets on land which had been soaking in salt water for 600 years. Incidentally, the polders to be started later would benefit from the gradual sweetening of the IJsselmeer, which would leach out much of the salt left behind by the Zuider Zee.

By 1929 the test polder was dry, and the next task was to make the soil useful. In the past, at the German end of the North Sea, land had been reclaimed from the sea by impolder-

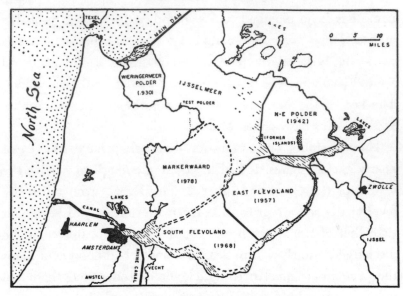

49. The polders in the former Zuider Zee

ing, too. There, a rule of thumb among the peasants had been
that a new polder, if kept well drained, would become useful in
six or seven years' time. In half a dozen years enough rain fell on
a polder to wash the salt away. The Dutch presumably had done
the same in the past, but now they were looking for methods to
speed up the natural process. Gypsum was added to the soil,
then fertilizers—different fertilizers in different parts of the test
polder. Then the men experimented with various vegetables to
see which crop would be the first to succeed on such soil. The
test polder ceased to exist as such on November 1, 1935. It had
done its job as an experimental farm; now it became a regular
farm.

By that time the main dam was finished.

The island of Wieringen served as an anchor. It had been
connected to the mainland with a comparatively short dam in

1925. The big job was building the dam from Wieringen to Friesland—20 miles of dam to be built right through the sea. The
bulk of the dam is sand and earth dredged from the sea bottom.
On the inland side the dam has a heavy stone facing; on the
seaward side there is a bulge of boulder clay. On top of this
clay were laid brushwood mattresses, made by twisting brushwood into heavy ropelike shapes and then weaving these "ropes"
into mattresses on top of which the workers dumped heavy
boulders, field stones, pieces of old concrete—anything with
enough weight to withstand the pounding of the waves for an
indefinite length of time.

At first the job represented only hard work; large quantities
of clay and rocks had to be moved and put into position. But as
the building of the dam progressed the work seemed worth-
while, for the space through which the tide could flow in and
out of the Zuider Zee became narrower and narrower, and the
current in the remaining gap became more and more violent.
The man who furnished the necessary calculations for what to
expect of this current was Hendrick Antoon Lorentz, Nobel
Prize winner in physics in 1902. As the critical period of closing
the final gap approached, the expenditure in men and equipment began to resemble that for a battle. Ten thousand people
worked on the dam. There were 27 large dredges in action, 13
floating cranes, 132 barges, and 88 tugs. The closing of the dam

50. Cross section of the main dam across the mouth of the former
Zuider Zee

was timed, like a military attack. At a certain time the current was almost completely halted; then there were a certain number of hours for plugging the dam. When the tide returned a solid obstacle must halt it.

The dam was finished on May 28, 1932.

At that time the polder to the south of what had been the island of Wieringen, the Wieringermeer Polder, was ready to receive its first crop. Since the area was somewhat protected by the island (and the beginnings of the big dam) this polder had been finished in 1932, and the experience gained on the test polder enabled the Dutch experts to make the land arable within only two years of its being dry. On this polder—as well as on those finished later—the system was to divide it into plots of roughly 50 acres. Each one of these plots had a paved road in front of it and a large canal behind it, making it accessible both by land and by water. In case the main dam gave way, a most unlikely event, a *terp* (artificial hill) was built in the center of the polder. It is high enough to be several feet above the highest recorded flood level of the North Sea and large enough to protect everything on the polder that can climb it.

Two years after the big dam was finished, work began on the Northeast Polder which was ready to bear crops ten years later, in 1942. Naturally the soil of such a polder is not uniform; as anywhere else, the quality varies from area to area. The best land of a polder is used for vegetables, the next best for grain (mainly rye), while the poorest sections are forested.

As for the largest of the polders, formerly the Southeast Polder, now Flevoland, the phase called East Flevoland was ready in 1957; South Flevoland is expected to be ready in 1968. The Markerwaard Polder is expected to be ready in 1978.

When the Dutch started working on this enormous project in 1927 they probably expected, or at least hoped, that they could reclaim their Zuider Zee area in about half a century without having to worry about many other things. But two major catastrophes happened. The first was the German occupation of the Netherlands during the Second World War which, naturally, brought everything nearly to a standstill, though the Germans at first did not interfere directly. In fact, a number of German engineers investigated the Wieringermeer Polder, very carefully, if unofficially, because they had had a similar project in mind since about 1932. There had been talk about impoldering a bay called the *Frisches Haff* (east of Danzig) and the Germans wanted to see how such work was done. The Frisches Haff project would have been easier than that of the Zuider Zee for several reasons: to begin with the bay is nearly fresh water naturally, and, because of the geometry of the land, only an eight-mile dam would be needed. This project, incidentally, is now dead, because the area became Polish after the war, but, of course, it may be revived as a Polish project.

Near the end of the war, however, the Germans wrecked dikes deliberately to protect their own retreat, especially in the province of Zeeland. But the dikes wrecked by the retreating German armies were repaired, and Zeeland lived up to its Latin motto *luctor et emergo*, meaning "I struggle and emerge."

After the damage had been repaired, most Dutchmen, including the Zeelanders, would admit that such things could and would happen during a war, but that otherwise everything was fine with the dikes and the coexistence of the North Sea and the Kingdom of the Netherlands. The events which taught them differently occurred on the first day of February 1953. Storm conditions were unusually intense; the dikes of Zeeland were breached in sixty-seven places; 375,000 acres of land were flooded; and 9000 buildings were destroyed and 38,000 more damaged. The number of people dead reached 1800. The over-all damage was estimated at over 300 million dollars.

A Dutch agency, the *Rijkswaterstaat* (we would call an equivalent agency, if we had one, the Federal Water Administration) had been worried all along and had drafted memoranda about preventive measures that should be taken. But their warnings had appeared unnecessary; not counting the artificial wartime flooding, there had been no serious flood for a century. Also, their proposals had been very expensive. But after the February flood in 1953, every Dutchman suddenly realized what he had once learned in public school; namely, that 60 per cent of the kingdom's population lives and works below sea level. The Rijkswaterstaat's plan was quickly accepted.

Zeeland, as a glance at the map will show, consists of half a dozen large and a few small islands grouped around four major outlets for river water into the sea. But under bad storm conditions these become four major inlets for the sea. To insure the safety of the islands of Zeeland as they now are, some 500 miles of dikes would have to be raised six to seven feet, involving the reconstruction of about a hundred locks, culverts, pumping stations, and so forth. The alternative, the Delta Plan, is merely to tie the whole complex of islands together into one land area by building a total of about 20 miles of dikes as sturdy as the main dam across the mouth of the Zuider Zee.

The first step of the Delta Plan—now underway—is the so-called three-island plan, a name which is based on the fact that Walcheren, North Beveland, and South Beveland were once

51. The dams of the Delta Plan, with the dates of expected completion

three islands. Earlier work has already connected Walcheren and South Beveland. The dam across Haringvliet, the northernmost of the outlets bordering the nearby islands, is to be finished by 1968. Then the second outlet, the Brouwershavensche Gat, is to be dammed; this dam should be completed in 1970. The next dam, and incidentally the longest one in the Delta Plan, will go across the outlet called the *Easter Schelde* (it is called "Easter" not in reference to the religious holiday but geographically in relation to the *Wester Schelde*) and will seal it off by 1978. The southernmost of the outlets, the Wester Schelde, must be left open, as there is heavy traffic up and down this body of water to Antwerp, which is not a Dutch city. Here the dike along the southern shore of Walcheren and South Beveland will have to be raised and strengthened. The same is true to the north of Zeeland. The deep channel between Rotterdam and the sea, the so-called *Rotterdamsche Waterweg*, also cannot be interfered with, so a protecting dike at or near the southern shore of the waterway is indicated.

One of the reasons the Delta Plan was accepted so rapidly and has been pursued energetically is that, after careful examination of the storm conditions of 1953, it was discovered, to everybody's horror, that the situation still contained mitigating factors. The flood could have been four feet higher than it was!

The Delta Plan is mainly defensive; it is not aimed at producing much new land. But it has the secondary aim of producing a large fresh-water reservoir. The interconnected bodies of water behind the Delta Plan dams are already referred to collectively as the *Zeeuwse Meer,* the Zeeland Lake.

The fact is that the Netherlands, always plagued by too much sea water and also seasonally plagued by too much river water, does need more fresh water in midsummer. The Zeeuwse Meer will be used as an irrigation reservoir for these periods. During normal times the water from this body will go through a canal into the Rotterdamsche Waterweg in order to push the salt water which normally fills it out into the sea. Then the waterway could supply the farms along its banks with fresh water.

There are two secondary dams: from Duiveland to Overflakkee and from there to the mainland. Later on they will carry highways, but their primary purpose is to influence the currents in such a way that the main dams will be easier to build. Another part of the Delta Plan is an interesting construction to the east of Rotterdam. A river which flows into this region from the east is called the *Hollandsche IJssel;* despite its name it has no relation to the IJssel which puts fresh water into the IJssel-meer and which is sometimes called the *Geldersche IJssel* to avoid possible confusion of the two rivers. The Hollandsche IJssel represents a vulnerable point in case of a bad flood. The sea, racing up in a tidal wave through the Rotterdamsche Water-weg could enter the Hollandsche IJssel and pour into the low-lying land east of Rotterdam. What has been built is actually an enormous guillotine, a steel blade as wide as the river, rest-ing in two massive towers. If a wave should come up the waterway, the steel blade can be lowered within minutes, literally cutting off the flood.

As has been mentioned, the purpose of the Delta Plan is not to make more land, but to make the existing land safe. And, of course, the Delta Plan must be hurried as much as is feasible since nobody can foretell just when the next bad flood may take place, though there now may be an earlier advance warning because of the meteorological satellites (such as Tiros) in the sky. Still, the Delta Plan will result in reclaiming an ad-ditional 25,000 to 40,000 acres as a by-product.

However, there is a place where again as much land can be reclaimed as was gained by the impoldering of the Zuider Zee. A glance at the map shows the site. The North Sea is quite shallow north of the big Zuider Zee dam—this area is locally known as the Wadden Zee. North of the Wadden Zee there is a chain of islands, obviously indicating the original coastline. A dam from North Holland to the island of Texel would not be longer than the average Delta Plan dam although it might be more difficult to build. The same statement is true for the dams connecting the islands all the way to the island of Ameland, and a dam from Ameland to the mainland would be only about half the length of the Zuider Zee dam.

Questions about impoldering the Wadden Zee receive cautious official answers, such as: "No, there is no 'plan' yet." However, some experts are indubitably thinking private and unofficial thoughts about it. The official reluctance to say much is, in part, due to the fact that it would not be wise to start a new project until the Delta Plan is completed. The caution also may be based on the concern of the Dutch government for the purses and feelings of the Dutch taxpayers. But private experts can be, and are, less reluctant. A Dutch professor named Thysse has gone on record saying, "It will be done not later than the year 2000." It seems much more likely that it will be finished long before that date.

And it is quite certain that the Dutch will find a treasure ship in the process. It is known to be there but, unfortunately, "there" is a place within an area with a diameter of a mile or two, and nobody can tell how deep the sand is that covers the wreck.

This is what happened. The merchants and shippers of Hamburg were doing a flourishing business in 1798, but their business had expanded so rapidly that they had run short of ready cash. Hence, they requested a loan from London banks, and the bankers were very glad to oblige; it was a safe investment—or so it seemed. In October 1799, the sum requested by the Hamburg merchants, 24 million dollars, was ready in London mostly in gold coins, and the remainder in gold and silver bars which could be minted into coins in Hamburg. Since such a large amount of money was involved, the British government agreed to transport the money in a man-of-war, and the ship chosen was the *Lutine,* a well-armed and fast frigate, originally built by the French but taken by the English as a prize of war. The *Lutine,* weighed down with gold, set sail in the evening of October 9, 1799.

During the early morning hours of the next day, when the *Lutine* was nearly in sight of Helgoland, a storm developed, blowing her back toward Holland. The *Lutine* ran aground on a sand spit near the island of Terschelling and capsized. All but two of her three-hundred-man crew perished in the high seas. When the story became known, the Dutch government declared the sunken ship to be the property of the Netherlands. I do not know how the Hamburg merchants managed without the loan; as far as the English banks were concerned they were safe since the voyage of the *Lutine* had been insured with Lloyd's of London. The Dutch government had a windfall of 24 million dollars, but it was on the bottom of the Wadden Zee and had to be recovered.

The wreck of the *Lutine* was then still visible at low tide, and Dutch fishermen, working for the government, extracted about a million dollars worth of coins and metal bars by means of long-handled nets and oyster forks. But during the winter of 1801–2 currents buried the ship under many feet of sand. Everything to do with the ship since then has made one long story of frustration. During the years from 1857 to 1866 the *Lutine* became accessible again, but only about one million dollars worth of coins could be recovered. In 1911 another attempt was made; again enough was recovered to keep the optimists in good cheer and to prove that the wreck at the bottom actually was that of the *Lutine.*

Since then the *Lutine* has been talked about frequently, but there has been no recent success—the ship is again buried by sand.

But when the Wadden Zee is reclaimed, the *Lutine* will be reclaimed too.

11. RUSSIAN ENGINEERS DREAM, TOO

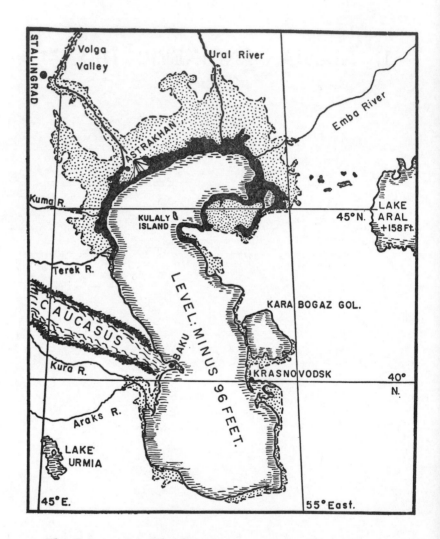

52. The Caspian Sea. The dotted area to the north of the sea is dry land below sea level; the dark area is land which has dried up since 1945

Russian Engineers Dream, Too

While Dutch engineers have performed miracles in building dams which keep water *out*, their Russian counterparts are contemplating dams to keep water *in*.

Naturally an area the size of Russia is bound to have a number of problems in which engineering science may prove helpful, but the two big problems concern the Caspian Sea and the Volga River. Nor are these two separate problems: they are linked, because most of the water received by the Caspian Sea comes from the Volga.

The Caspian Sea is the world's largest landlocked body of water, but it is only one of three remnants of a still larger sea which once existed in that area. Geologists call that sea the "Sarmatian Sea," and its area comprised the present Black Sea, the present Caspian Sea, and the present Lake Aral, which is over 200 miles east of the Caspian Sea. But the Sarmatian Sea extended much farther north and west than any of its three remnants of today. There is evidence that the Hungarian plain was once covered by the waters of this sea, but since much of the water must have been shallow, there obviously were large-scale fluctuations in its extent. These variations must have been similar to those of the present Lake Tchad in Africa—also the remnant of a former, much larger "sea"—for which every survey gives a different area. All the surveys are, as far as one can tell, correct, depending on how wet the preceding seasons were.

It is not yet known—although Soviet geologists are probably busy trying to establish this fact—just how the Sarmatian Sea fared during the time when much of northern Europe was covered by glaciers. It probably shrank in area then, to grow again when, after the last glaciation, much of the water that had been stored as snow and ice gradually returned to circulation. The major change came at a time still to be determined, when the western end of the Sarmatian Sea broke through to the Mediterranean. There is, as has been told on p. 146, a steady flow from the Black Sea into the Mediterranean even now. The flow rate probably was much higher when the connection between the Sarmatian Sea and the thirsty Mediterranean was first established. In any event, this connection spelled the end of the Sarmatian Sea, leaving bodies of water in only three especially deep depressions.

The westernmost of these three, the Black Sea, is doing relatively well as can be seen from the fact that it still supplies water to the Mediterranean. The easternmost of the three, Lake Aral, is also in good shape. With an area of 26,200 square miles it is slightly smaller than Lake Victoria in Africa which it resembles in shape. Its level is now 158 feet above sea level, and its maximum measured depth is 222 feet. Its area seems to have been stable for centuries; its level has risen a little during the last fifty years. Of course, if an earthquake opened a chasm in a westerly direction leading to the depression of the Caspian Sea, the lake that would be left would have hardly any resemblance to "blue Lake Aral" of today. Although its maximum measured depth is 222 feet, the average depth is somewhere between 55 and 65 feet; if a drainage to about sea level were opened, very little would be left of the lake.

If it can be said that the Black Sea is "doing well" and that Lake Aral is "in good shape," no such statement can be made about the central depression of the old Sarmatian Sea, the Caspian Sea. Its level is by now 96 feet *below* sea level and is still sinking. Even with these handicaps it is the largest "lake," if that term is used to denote a body of water not connected with the oceans. If saltiness is the criterion used, the Caspian is a "sea"; the average figure for the whole Caspian reads .22 ounces of salt per quart of water. (For the Atlantic Ocean the figure is 1.23 ounces per quart.) In reality the "average" does not apply; in the north, say, north of the 45th parallel, the water is drinkable. Logically, it is less salty than the average in the south. The bay of Kara Bogaz Gol is a very special case which needs separate description.

The dimensions of the Caspian are impressive: from north to south it stretches for nearly 800 miles, and the widest part measures 275 miles across. The area is about 169,000 square miles, two-thirds of which is deeper than 600 feet, and two-thirds of that deep section is in the southernmost part, south of the line from Baku to Krasnovodsk. The third city of noticeable size in this region, in addition to the two just mentioned, is Astrakhan in the north, near the delta of the Volga.

The water supply of the Caspian Sea comes from two major rivers, the Volga and the Ural, and five minor ones—Emba, Kuma, Terek, Kura, and Araks. Of the minor rivers the Terek looks major in late spring when it is swollen by the melting snows of the Caucasus. All together they carry 175 cubic miles of water into the Caspian every year—after all the Volga is Europe's largest river—but this makes up for the loss of water through evaporation only in very wet years. The Caspian, like the Mediterranean, lies in a usually warm and almost always dry climate. Dry winds coming from Asia in the east make the evaporation rate equal to the influx, even though the annual influx is as great as the volume of Lake Erie.

One of the main reasons for the loss is a strange bay, Kara Bogaz Gol. Its area is about 7100 square miles—for comparison, the area of Lake Ontario is 7540 square miles—with a maximum depth of 40 feet and an average depth of about 5 feet. The channel connecting the bay with the Caspian is roughly one mile in length and not much over 400 feet wide on the average. Through this channel pass 22,000 cubic feet of water per second, to be evaporated in this natural salt pan. Since the minerals carried into the bay can only return to the Caspian to the same extent as the water which carried them—namely, not at all— the end result is that the general salinity of the Caspian is kept rather low while that of the bay is fantastically high. An estimated 1000 million tons of minerals—impure Epsom salts, to be specific—cover the bottom of the bay, in some places to a depth of 7 feet.

To this list of seemingly incredible data, I can add another equally surprising fact. In the bay of Krasnovodsk, just south of the Epsom-salts bay, the inhabitants often hunt seals!

In the north the fisheries are somewhat more conservative; there the fishermen catch salmon, herring, and sturgeon. The catch of the latter—90 per cent of all sturgeon are caught in the Caspian—has a decisive bearing on the caviar trade. But it is just this caviar corner of the Caspian which is shrinking at a literally visible rate. Most of the small fishing towns are now miles from shore. And even though each foot of recession produces nearly 100,000 acres of arable land the over-all picture results in a loss. The Soviets say that the Caspian Sea now costs them a billion rubles per year,* and they don't pretend to be unconcerned about it. Part of the shrinkage is due, strangely enough, to the main water supplier of the Caspian, the Volga. From more than two hundred mouths the Volga pours about four times as much water into the Caspian Sea as all the other rivers together. But with the water come 55 million cubic feet of sediments annually—more if the spring flood of the Volga has been exceptionally high. The deposit of the sediments makes the northern section, the fishing grounds, shallow. For many years steamers were aware of the fact that they had to lighten cargo if they wished to pass the Volga Delta at a distance closer than 40 miles. What makes the 55 million cubic feet of sediment even more deplorable to Russian economists is that a large percentage of it once was good topsoil along the river's course. Whatever good land may be gained from the Caspian's recession simply had been lost elsewhere at an earlier time.

This recession of the Caspian Sea is not a novelty. During the fourteenth century somebody tried to determine its level as best as could be done with the means then available. Expressed in our measurements, the result was that the level of the Caspian was 50 feet below sea level. Comparing this figure to a measurement carried out in 1900 the result is that the level of the Caspian had dropped between seven and eight feet per century.

---

* This statement was made before the exchange rate of the ruble was increased, hence the annual expenditures are the equivalent of 200 to 250 million dollars.

But just about 1900 the rate of recession began to increase. The average temperature of that area has risen by about 2 degrees Fahrenheit. This meant not only higher evaporation losses the year round but also less water supply. The Volga lost more water by evaporation before the Caspian was reached, and other rivers carried less water to begin with, especially those from the Caucasus where the snow line moved up so that there was less snow and ice to melt in the spring. Finally, during the last few years, the hydroelectric activities of the Russians have withheld Volga water, too. The large artificial lake to the north of the power dam at Kuibyshev has an area of 1900 miles and filling it up required all the water of the spring flood of 1957.

The level of the Caspian dropped by eight feet between 1930 and 1960, and for the decade from 1960 to 1970 a drop of *at least* three more feet is expected.

Naturally the Russians are asking themselves what they can do about it; they don't like their annual billion-ruble loss. One simple and obvious suggestion is to dam the outlet into the Kara Bogaz Gol. It would save 5184 million cubic feet of water per month. This amount sounds large, but it would not make too much difference as far as the whole body of the Caspian Sea is concerned. In fact, if the inlet is ever dammed, it would not be to save water but to facilitate the exploitation of the mineral deposits at the bottom of that bay.

A suggestion, made by the oceanographer B. A. Apollov, is not concerned with the Caspian Sea as a whole but with the northern portion, which is of economic importance because of the fisheries. Apollov's suggestion amounts to splitting the Caspian into two bodies of water by means of a dam.

The distance from the mouth of the Kuma River to the island

of Kulaly is 280 miles. If a dam would be built across the Caspian
Sea from the west shore to Kulaly Island and from the island to
a convenient point on the east shore, the valuable northern portion would be separated from the southern portion, which is
without fisheries of any consequence. The waters coming from
the Volga, the Ural, the Emba, and the Kuma would then all
remain in the northern portion. This would tend to make the
water of this section fresher though for most practical purposes
it is fresh water right now. It would put the fishermen back into
their normal occupation. It would avoid expensive dredging for
the approaches to the northern ports, especially Astrakhan,
which now has to be done all the time. And, of course, the dam
could have several lock gates in convenient places so that
the shipping could go on from the north to the south and
vice versa.

Apollov's suggestion is not yet a "plan" and certainly not yet
a "project." It would require a great number of preliminary surveys to establish the type of dam, the method of construction,
and even the line which could be followed most efficiently across
the sea. That a 280-mile dam through shallow water is an
engineering possibility cannot be doubted. What it would cost
is another problem, but anything that can help to avoid an
annual billion-ruble loss is worth looking into from a Russian
viewpoint. It seems to be the simplest way to save the fisheries,
including the caviar trade.

Apollov's dam would solve the Caspian Sea problem, but
so far the Soviet authorities do not seem to have done anything
about it; quite possibly they want to see how their "Greater
Volga Plan" is going to influence the situation. This plan will
make it possible for the Caspian Sea to receive some river water

which would not flow into it naturally. Part of the Greater Volga Plan involves making a canal from the Don to the Volga— a project which Czar Peter the Great had in mind in his day and which was actually started by him though it had to be abandoned. The project was simply too big for its time; moreover, a Don-Volga canal without pumping stations would be an impossibility because of intervening hills. In the current project the Don water has to be lifted 150 feet, but from there the drop into the Volga is 300 feet.

The Volga is Europe's longest river (2300 miles—the same length as the Yukon), and it has always been the pride of the Russians. But it also has always been a very difficult river, as can be seen from a few simple figures. Of the total amount of water the Volga brings to the Caspian Sea during the year only 13 per cent arrives during the four winter months. Summer and fall together account for 15 to 20 per cent, while between 60 and 70 per cent of the total arrives during the six weeks of high water during the spring. The Volga either flooded the countryside or showed a tendency to disappear.

That "something should be done" has been recognized since about 1850 but the measures taken at that time consisted in the building of levees which proved effective only when Nature happened to cooperate. It was not a problem that could be solved by man power and sandbags.

In 1927 the Soviet government ordered a full-scale study of the Volga's misbehavior which involved all the ramifications of water utilization. The difference in levels from the source of the river to its delta is 845 feet. Between Rybinsk and Shcherbakov (where the Volga has become a large river) and Astrakhan it is still 430 feet. Utilization of this level difference for hydroelectric power was one aspect. Another was the fact that, lower down, there is a belt of fertile land, about 300 miles wide and close to 1000 miles long, at the left bank of the Volga. Or rather, this land would be very fertile if it had received water from the Volga when necessary. Under natural conditions it usually did not. The next aspect was the prevention of flooding in the spring. Finally, there was the desirability of connecting the Volga with other rivers, not only the Don, but also the Ural, and the Moskva River on which Moscow is situated.

After five years of study and planning, the Greater Volga Plan was officially approved. The total plan involves thirteen hydroelectric power plants, three major canals, and countless irrigation projects.

The first hydroelectric power plant on the Volga proper is the one called Shcherbakov, near the city of that name. The artificial lake of Rybinsk connects to the south with two more power plants, Uglich and Ivankovo. The Volga-Moskva canal begins below the Ivankovo power dam; there are no additional dams along this stretch. Now the Moskva River, east of the city of Moscow, joins the Oka, which in turn is a tributary of the Volga, their confluence being marked by the city named after the novelist Maxim Gorki. The second power dam along the Volga is at Gorki. The Volga flows more or less due east after Gorki, producing a 60-foot drop before turning south. This drop is utilized in the power dam of Tcheboksary. Beyond the dam the Volga turns south and is then soon joined by the Kama River, a river not too well known to Americans but a big river, nevertheless.

Above the junction with the Volga there are to be three power dams across the Kama River, the northernmost named Verkhne

Kamskaya, the next one simply Kamskaya (near the city of Molotov), and the third one Votkinsk. At the junction of the two rivers there is the Nishne Kamskaya power dam followed by the one near the city of Kuibyshev which apparently is going to be the largest of them all. Between Kuibyshev and Volgograd there is one more power dam, at Saratov. The last power dam on the Volga is that of Volgograd, a short distance north of the city. Just north of that power dam the Volga-Ural canal branches, and just below the city of Volgograd the Volga-Don canal branches. Between there and the Caspian Sea there are no additional dams, but the Don River will have a big one northeast of Rostov.

This is the Greater Volga Plan. It is not finished yet by any means, but it is underway.

At a later date the Greater Volga Plan is to be augmented by the "turn-about" of three rivers which empty into the Arctic Ocean west of the Ural mountains. From west to east they are (1) the Dvina with the important port of Archangel at its mouth, (2) the Mezen River which is the smallest of the three, and (3) the Pechora River which is the largest.

The current idea is to dam the Pechora—which, if the plan is carried out, would be the first project to be tackled—near a place called Ust Shagor. This site is rather far upstream, and the Pechora receives a number of important tributaries farther downstream so that the river as a whole would not disappear; it would merely carry less water. The waters of the upper Pechora could be backed up into the Kama River and thus into the Volga. Similar measures could also add the waters of the Mezen and the Dvina to the Volga, which is the center of all this planning.

The big Russian projects, those actually under construction and those with a reasonable chance of being started within the next decade, are all in European Russia where the population density is highest. If the projects are completed, the general picture on the map will not look too different from a map picture of 1900. But the major volume of the waters of some of the rivers will flow south instead of north, the rivers which flow south naturally will no longer flood, and the Caspian Sea, the Russians hope, will have become a stable body of water.

Epilogue

I am well aware of the fact that I haven't said a word about space travel, which is an engineer's dream too. I haven't said anything about space travel in this book for the simple reason that I have said many words about it elsewhere, in *Rockets, Missiles and Space Travel* and in *The Exploration of Mars*, written in conjunction with Wernher von Braun.

I haven't said a word about atomic energy either, except by way of explanation of how the sun keeps going. Here the reason is somewhat different. Though atomic energy began in the physicist's laboratory it was developed first for military purposes. Under the exigencies of war the possible peacetime uses had to wait, but it was expected all along that such peacetime uses would come to the fore. The expectation was well founded, there are now various types of nuclear reactors for the purpose of producing power.

The most important atomic "fuel," as is well known, is uranium. In its pure form uranium is a metal which looks very much like silver but is almost as heavy as gold. Every uranium nucleus holds 92 protons, subatomic particles with a positive electric charge. And the normal uranium nucleus also holds 146 neutrons, subatomic particles which are electrically neutral. But a small number of uranium atoms, 1 in every 140, hold only 143 neutrons apiece. (An even rarer form, about 1 in 5000, holds only 142 neutrons in each atom.) Chemically, because of the 92 protons, these atoms are all uranium, but "atomically" they differ. The more common form has a total nuclear mass of $92 + 146 = 238$ and is therefore called uranium-238 or U-238. The rarer form ("isotope" is the technical term) has a mass of $92 + 143 = 235$. This is U-235, which can and will "fission," that is, split into smaller atoms with a release of energy. U-238 does not fission, but in an atomic reactor U-238, or some of it, might be transformed into elements with an even bigger nucleus than uranium —into plutonium, for example, which will fission like U-235.

All along it has seemed as if it might be possible to make an atomic reactor which would not only release energy while it operated but also would produce, at the expense of the normally inert U-238, more fissionable material than was put into it when it was started. The breeder-reactor is that device. It works. Here is a means of actually creating "fuel," not from nothing, of course, but from something which is not a fuel.

Another way of obtaining atomic fuel is based on another nuclear transformation, that of changing thorium-232 into uranium-233. And it has been demonstrated that another of the heavy-weight isotopes can be made to yield power, though in a somewhat roundabout way. There is a plutonium isotope, namely plutonium-238, which has been considered as "atomic ash" ever since it became known. It does not fission, but it is radioactive, and if a certain (undisclosed) amount of plutonium-238 is kept in a container it will slowly grow hot, and *stay* hot, because of its natural radioactivity. Utilizing this fact, engineers inserted a thermocouple into the lump of plutonium-238, with the result that one end of this thermocouple is permanently heated. The power output of the device is 25 watts and its name is SNAP 9-A (*Systems for Nuclear Auxiliary Power*, type 9-A). Its purpose is to power artificial satellites and, possibly, automatic weather stations in remote areas.

Unusual natural resources like nuclear transformations and the utilization of the heat of naturally radioactive substances were uncovered by means of another natural resource—never specifically mentioned in all the discussions but probably the most important one of all—our own ingenuity.

INDEX

Index

(Figures in italics refer to illustrations and diagrams. A figure followed by *n* refers to a footnote.)